Beat Transnationalism

John Tytell

Published by Beatdom Books

Also by John Tytell

Writing Beat and Other Occasions of Literary Mayhem, Vanderbilt University Press, 2014.

The Beat Interviews, Beatdom Books, 2014.

Reading New York, Alfred A. Knopf, 2003.

Paradise Outlaws: Remembering the Beats, William Morrow/ Harper Collins: New York, 1999. Photographs by Mellon.

The Living Theatre: Art, Exile and Outrage, Grove Press: New York, 1995.

Passionate Lives: D.H. Lawrence, F. Scott Fitzgerald, Henry Miller, Dylan Thomas, Sylvia Plath--In Love, Birch Lane Press: Carol Publishers, New York, 1991.

Ezra Pound: The Solitary Volcano. Doubleday: New York, 1987.

Naked Angels: Lives and Literature of the Beat Generation. McGraw-Hill, 1976.

Dedicated to Mellon,
        My Wife and Muse,
            the recipient of all my love letters.

Published by Beatdom Books

Copyright © 2017 by John Tytell

Cover photograph © 2017 Mellon Tytell

Author photograph © 2017 Mellon Tytell

Both photos taken in Oaxaca, 1974.

All rights reserved. No part of this book may be reproduced in any form or by any electronic or mechanical means including information storage and retrieval systems, without permission in writing from the author. The only exception is by a reviewer, who may quote short excerpts in a review.

View the publisher's website:
www.books.beatdom.com

First Print Edition
ISBN 978-0-9934099-1-2

Table of Contents

Preface: Crossing Boundaries..i

I. The Mexican Magnet..1

II. The Oaxaca Letters..40

III. The Triumvirate: Ginsberg, Kerouac, Burroughs..........117

    1- Howl@60..119
    2- Ginsberg's Farm..133
    3- The Kerouac Conundrum: A Reputation Study..........139
    4- Transnational Beat......................................155

IV. Messengers..169

    5- Bonnie Bremser's Mexico..............................171
    6 - Judith Malina at the Barricades......................183
    7- Patti Smith's Matchbox................................195

V. Artisans and Impresarios..................................201

    8- Laughlin's Literary Lost Souls........................203
    9- Renegade Rosset..209
    10- Ferlinghetti's Walkabout..............................219

Since I have returned from America one of those revolutions that shake the human race has broken out in the Spanish Colonies, and promises a new future for the 14 million inhabitants spread out from La Plata to the remotest areas in Mexico. Deep resentments, exacerbated by colonial laws and maintained by suspicious policies, have stained with bloodshed areas that for three centuries once enjoyed not happiness but at least uninterrupted peace.

[…]

What we glean from travellers' vivid descriptions has a special charm; whatever is far off and suggestive excites our imagination; such pleasures tempt us far more than anything we may daily experience in the narrow circle of sedentary life.

Alexander von Humboldt, *Personal Narrative*

Preface:

Crossing Boundaries

In 1974, I received a National Endowment for the Humanities Fellowship to work on *Naked Angels*, a book that would be the first to account for the development of the Beat Generation. I could not continue teaching while benefiting from the grant, but I also could not easily afford to continue living in New York on it.

One of the subjects of my inquiry in *Naked Angels* was the poet, Allen Ginsberg, who around that time remarked that I would never fully understand the members of his generation until I first experienced Mexico. Although I was married, my wife, Mellon, decided not to accompany me to Oaxaca—she was working in New York and wanted her freedom, and I needed space.

Naked Angels was published by McGraw-Hill in 1976, which then still had a large trade division. The book was reviewed widely and receptively. Reviewers in *The New York Times* and *The New Yorker* agreed that the book established a credibility for the Beats that had not existed previously. A decade later, when McGraw-Hill discontinued its trade division, Barney Rosset at

Grove Press picked the book up and kept it in print for another two decades. There were also a number of foreign editions. Remarkably, the book has never been out of print in the United States.

Last summer, while organizing a personal archive, I discovered a cache of some fifty long letters I wrote to Mellon from Oaxaca, Mexico during that period. As I began to read them, I realized the letters formed a sort of anthropological trove, the impressions of Mexico—then very much still a third-world country—of an innocent American whose views were maturing due to exposure and exploration. As an epistolary diary, the letters were my only way of communicating with my wife, but they also exist in a vital literary dimension as I try to come to terms with the dilemmas of composition, an unresponsive editor, the particularly vexing issues presented by the Beats, and the material I was reading on Mexico.

My first focus in this book is the impact of Mexico on the Beats and the letters should be considered as its emotional core. While living in Oaxaca, I studied Spanish for the first early dawn hour every day, and when I had leisure time I read what I could to help understand the Mexican experience—novels like Malcolm Lowry's *Under the Volcano*, collections like D. H. Lawrence's *Mornings In Mexico*, travel journals like Lawrence Ferlinghetti's *The Mexican Night*.

These letters were written forty years ago during a period of marital separation on an Olivetti typewriter—that now forgotten medium—and they were in their way expressions of love and an attempt to comprehend what had driven us apart, and what I needed to understand about myself to bring us together again. Actually, fate played an intervening role. My wife is a photographer and *The Magazine of Natural History* asked her to photograph the Zapotec Indians in the Oaxaca valley and their flower cultivation. The story has a happy ending because we rejoined and remain united.

The subject of the Beats in Mexico continued to resonate with me as the essay here on Bonnie Bremser might suggest. A few years ago I was asked by the Americas Society in

Manhattan to speak on this issue, and the result was "The Mexican Magnet" essay which begins this book. "Howl," the first public announcement of a new generational sensibility, had in part been precipitated by Ginsberg's own experience in Mexico, and when I wrote an essay re-evaluating that poem on the sixtieth anniversary of its publication, I knew I was on the way to another book.

In 2015, Lawrence Ferlinghetti's travel journals were published, and I realized that, for the Beats, Mexico had been a door opening to the rest of the American continent and beyond. Their search was transnational as well as multicultural, as many of these essays suggest. I have chosen to include essays on Judith Malina and Patti Smith, as one indication of how women were active participants in spreading the Beat message. Other essays, like the ones on Kerouac and the publishers James Laughlin, Barney Rosset, and Ferlinghetti, are broadly related to the issues I am exploring and they are recent.

Several issues reverberate through these essays, beginning with the importance of the First Amendment to the U.S. Constitution, protecting freedom of speech. For the Beats, taste often represented a subtle means of censorship, a means of shielding society with the excuse of propriety from what were once inexpressible taboo subjects, like sex or drugs. For the Beats, crossing boundaries was never merely geographical but always culturally consequential, inevitably leading to new awareness. If their challenging of the status quo—what they saw as the suffocating straight-jacket of a particularly repressive and conformist decade after World War Two—led to what society regarded as transgression, then we can see their emphasis on movement and resulting flights more as steps in a search, unconventional or irregular at times, of a new consciousness.

I
The Mexican Magnet

> who disappeared into the volcanoes of Mexico leaving
> behind nothing but the shadows of dungarees
> and the ash and lava of poetry . . .
>
> Allen Ginsberg, "Howl"

Prologue

William Burroughs, Jack Kerouac, and Allen Ginsberg felt that they needed to leave their own culture in order to see it more clearly, and they were almost magnetically drawn south to Mexico. Each of these writers spent formative years in the early 1950s living in Mexico, and each was startled by the perspectives afforded by what Burroughs characterized as an "oriental culture." Mexico was still quite impoverished in the 1950s—Gulf oil development created a middle class there only in the 1960s. What these writers saw in Mexico, and the circumstances of their lives there (e.g., Kerouac's destitution and vagrancy, Burroughs' awareness that drugs would become the subject of his writing, and his fatal shooting of his common-law companion), would find reflections in Burroughs' novels like *Junky*, *Queer*, and *Naked Lunch*; Kerouac's *On the Road* and *Tristessa*; and living in Chiapas would lead to such poems by Ginsberg as the early "Siesta in Xbalba" and "Howl." Their respective views evolved as the result of what they experienced: at first, Burroughs saw Mexico as an opportune occasion for libertarianism, Kerouac imagined a pastoral idyll, and Ginsberg experienced a transformative place "beyond Darwin's chain." What seems quite clear is that Mexico affected the development of each of their own literary voices.

I. Murder and Morphine

In the immediate aftermath of World War II, there were a few young people with literary ambitions, full of a bottled eagerness to tell their stories, who would later be identified as "beat"— i.e. politically unaffiliated, suspicious of institutional ties, organizational structures and establishment values, vaguely bohemian, animated by youthful non-conforming impulses. Simultaneously, some of the members of this small group suffered from an existential, psychic exhaustion, a sense of being beaten down spiritually by what seemed to them the regimented and oppressive patterns of American life. Living in an historical period of what seemed stasis to them, their immediate priority became movement.

If the key figures in the Beat Generation—William Burroughs, Jack Kerouac, and Allen Ginsberg—would become known as transgressive innovators who crossed boundaries with what were then taboo subjects, like drugs or the sort of sadomasochistic sexuality dramatized in Burroughs' *Naked Lunch,* they were also driven to cross national boundaries from Latin America to North Africa and Asia. Deeply, on some inchoate, intuitive level, they felt they needed to leave their own

The Mexican Magnet

culture in order to see it, and themselves, more clearly, and early circumstances drew them almost magnetically to Mexico.

One register of the transformative, opening impact of Mexico for the Beats—the opportunity to "learn ourselves"—occurs near the end of *On the Road* when Jack Kerouac announces "the earth is an Indian thing." After a series of recklessly rollicking, cross-country trips, his protagonists finally reach Mexico. Kerouac's narrator, Sal Paradise, is driving "alone in [his] eternity at the wheel" and declares in a line of sweeping significance:

> Not like driving across Carolina, or Texas, or Arizona, or Illinois; but like driving across the world and into the places where we would finally learn ourselves among the Fellaheen Indians of the world, the essential strain of the basic primitive, wailing humanity that stretches in a belt around the equatorial belly of the world . . .

In the fall of 1944, seven years before Kerouac wrote those lines, William Burroughs had collaborated with Kerouac on *And the Hippos Were Boiled in Their Tanks,* a hard-boiled apprenticeship novel written in a style imitating Dashiell Hammett and Raymond Chandler. By then, Burroughs, Kerouac, Ginsberg, and two women were sharing a large apartment on a 115th Street, close to Columbia University.

The libertine circle that ensued was divided to what they called the Rimbaudians —beautiful, seducible innocents— and the Baudelaireans as jaded as Burroughs. Floating in and out of the apartment—a kind of new casual salon on the upper West Side of Manhattan—were a series of petty criminals and intellectuals who could have been invented by Oscar Wilde, Frederick Nietzsche, or Jean Genet. These young men, as the writer Seymour Krim once observed, were "living harder and more extensively than any of their articulate American counterparts."

And the Hippos Were Boiled in Their Tanks, which would only be published seventy years after its completion, was based on Lucian Carr's murder of David Kammerer. Kammerer had been Carr's former scoutmaster, and he had relentlessly pursued Carr to Columbia University, intent on convincing the younger man to become his lover. Kammerer was a childhood friend of Burroughs' and, like Carr, was part of an upper class, privileged enclave in St. Louis society.

A blonde, elfin young man, wiry and wily, projecting an imperious arrogance and an unconventional rebelliousness, Carr was a catalyst figure in the Beat circle because he had introduced Ginsberg and Kerouac to Burroughs. One night, in August of 1944, after a lot of alcohol, Kammerer had persuaded Carr to accompany him to the banks of the Hudson River where he attempted to sexually accost him. Carr defended himself with the scout knife he always carried, weighed Kammerer's body with rocks, and threw it into the river.

Eight years older than Kerouac and twelve years older than Ginsberg, Burroughs had already received a B.A. from Harvard and had done graduate work there as well. He had traveled in Europe, and had lived in Vienna as a medical student in 1937. His sophistication was partly a function of caste; his paternal grandfather had perfected the adding machine, leading to the Burroughs Corporation, a Fortune 500 company with skyscrapers in several cities. He had read a good deal more of modern literature than his new friends had—Kafka and T.S. Eliot, for example—and he introduced them to Oswald Spengler's *Decline and Fall of the West*, which was influential.

A more dangerous initiation than Spengler, though, was introduced by Herbert Huncke, a Times Square hustler and coat thief Burroughs had met. Huncke had arresting stories about his experiences as a child runaway and working with a circus. At some point in the early summer of 1944, he initiated Burroughs, Kerouac, and Ginsberg into the hipster's illuminated world with injections of morphine. Though neither Kerouac nor Ginsberg would become addicted, Burroughs did, along with his companion, a young woman named Joan Vollmer Adams, who had an infant daughter and a husband away fighting on the European front. Joan Vollmer developed a fatal attraction for

The Mexican Magnet

Burroughs and would conceive a son by him in a common-law union in 1947.

By then, Burroughs, Joan, and her infant daughter Julie Adams had left the 115th Street apartment. Burroughs had been apprehended after forging a medical prescription and although his family helped provide legal counsel, he became too paranoid to stay in New York. Instead, he purchased a ninety-acre spread in bayou country near New Waverly, Texas, fifty miles north of Houston. Between rows of cotton and alfalfa, he managed to grow and harvest a crop of poor quality marijuana, which he transported to Times Square and sold.

Again nervous because of traffic infractions and police visits—the neighbors, a mile away, complained of incessant shooting at Burroughs' farm—he moved to Algiers, a community just outside New Orleans, which provided access to drugs on which both he and Joan Vollmer had become dependent. The drugs affected his ethical understanding, as is evident in a letter he sent Ginsberg on November 30, 1948:

> "Crime" is simply behavior outlawed by a given culture . . . I do not see a connection between lying and violation of the law. In fact, there is more lying in the course of a "regular job" most of which require a constant state of pretense and dissimulation . . .

Almost all businessmen violated the law on a daily basis, Burroughs advised in his letter, sent a few weeks before another surprising encounter with police authority. The New Orleans police raided the Burroughs household—tipped off by the New Waverly authorities— and they discovered a cache of drugs and weapons. Unfortunately, they had failed to secure a proper warrant so the search was legally compromised. In the meantime, Burroughs and his family, including a son who had been born in New Waverly, fled to Mexico City.

II. Why Mexico?

Lâchez tout—abandon everything—the surrealist theoretician, Andre Breton, had advised his cohort in Paris in the early 1920s. Breton's radical prescription responded to what the French called "ennui," a quality of spiritual exhaustion comparable to what some of the Beats in New York felt after World War II. In a repeated image, the novelist, Henry Miller, called *lâchez tout* the "blind leap into the dark." It required the folly of a peculiar kind of courage, the drastic ability to depart suddenly from one's country, as Miller had in 1929, sacrificing family, career, routine expectations, domestic security, and comfort. In Breton's surrealist circle, voyage to a fundamentally different culture—Melville in the Marquesas Islands in 1842 or Antonin Artaud with the Tarahumara in Mexico nearly a century later—was considered a vital ingredient in any writer's sensibility that could lead to the freedom of an avant-garde perspective.

Initially, Burroughs' intention was to open a bar on the Mexican side of the border. He had worked as a bartender in Chicago and Manhattan, but surely he would have been the only bartender in Mexico with a Harvard degree. He had, however, conceived of the notion of buying land in Mexico to grow opium, which he had tried but failed to grow in Texas because the climate north of the Rio Grande was unsuitable. His ambition points to his transgressive nature, an extreme, unorthodox response to the settled complacency of American life in the 1950s.

The legality of this project did not trouble him. In letters to Allen Ginsberg, written in November and December of 1948, he explained that as a farmer in Texas, he had observed that the largest farmers were allowed to violate the law by importing seasonal Mexican labor—called "wetbacks" because they were often required to wade across the Rio Grande at night—frequently maintained in conditions of virtual slavery. The law, he rationalized, was only relative to the power of money. Burroughs maintained that there was more pretense, dissimulation, and misrepresentation in acceptable business practices like advertising, television, and public relations (a field which his uncle, Ivy Lee, pioneered) than in the sale of drugs.

Unfortunately for Burroughs, as a result of the Mexican War and what American politicians called "Manifest Destiny," and the subsequent annexation of most of the American southwest, Mexicans had made it very difficult for North Americans to own property in their own names. Usually, a Mexican attorney would secure a deed in his name and the American client might occupy the property, which would work out well with a villa in a tourist resort like Acapulco, but which seemed much less feasible if the plan was to purchase land to farm opium. Burroughs found an attorney and applied to formally obtain Mexican citizenship. After considerable expense, he became frustrated when the Mexican bureaucrats mysteriously lost his file.

Settling in Mexico City, Burroughs began classes in Mayan and Aztec archeology and civilization at Mexico City College, fascinated by the absolute control systems maintained by priestly castes over a millennium. Burroughs was taking advantage of available veterans' educational stipends, a monthly allowance of $75.00, plus books and tuition. He had been drafted during the war and summarily declared unfit for service, possibly for acknowledging his homosexual preferences. Supported by a modest family trust fund, he did not need the federal benefit, but, as he advised Kerouac with typical laconic acidity in a letter written on January 22, 1950, "I always say keep your snout in the public trough."

At first, Burroughs was happy in Mexico. He had seen a tripling of the federal bureaucracy in the United States after the end of World War II, and had chafed under agricultural controls when he was farming. In a letter to Kerouac in June, 1949, which contained a libertarian seed metaphor for *Naked Lunch*, he had complained that the officials who determined government agricultural quotas were a germinal "cancer on the political body of this country which no longer belongs to its citizens." In Mexico, there seemed to be less state control and governmental interference with daily activity. Even illegal drugs, needles, and syringes, for example, were available for very little money; doctors could be easily convinced to write prescriptions for morphine, and he could satisfy his heroin addiction for about a dollar a day.

As he neared the completion of *Junky*, the first novel he would write in Mexico, Burroughs remarked that he felt safe there from the antinarcotics propaganda that had been manufactured by American politicians and government officials:

> Initial symptoms of nationwide hysteria were clear. Louisiana passed a law making it a crime to be a drug addict. Since . . . the term "addict" is not clearly defined, no proof is necessary or even relevant under a law so formulated. No proof, and consequently, no trial. This is police-state legislation penalizing a state of being.

The absence of regulation was evident in the omnipresence of guns in Mexico City. If a policeman found a weapon, Burroughs observed, the worst that would probably happen is that he would seize it for resale. In his second novel, *Queer,* Burroughs argued that Mexican police were as respected as streetcar conductors, and were always susceptible to—the bribe they took to supplement their meager salary. He was particularly pleased when, for a modest fee, he obtained a permit to carry a pistol. According to Burroughs, life in Mexico was somewhat analogous to life on the American frontier as late as the 1880s.

In October, 1949, when Burroughs arrived in Mexico City, its population was approximately one million and the air seemed clean with "a special shade of blue that goes so well with circling vultures" as he observed in his 1985 introduction to *Queer*. He would associate the ominous, and particularly subjective, detail of circling vultures with Mexico and compound it several years later after fleeing the country, writing the beginning of *Naked Lunch*:

The Mexican Magnet

> Something falls off you when you cross the border into Mexico, and suddenly the landscape hits you straight with nothing between you and it, deserts and mountains and vultures; little wheeling specks and others so close you can hear wings cut the air (a dry husking sound), and when they spot something they pour out of the blue sky, that shattering bloody blue sky of Mexico, down in a black funnel.

"A single man lives high here including all the alcohol he wants to drink for $100 a month," Burroughs wrote to Kerouac in January of 1950, enticing him to visit. In fact, as Burroughs would later learn, when searching for the psychedelic vine ayahuasca (yagé) on the Putumayo River border region between Columbia and Peru, the closer the traveler came to the Equator, the less costly living expenses became, almost in direct proportion to the hazards for human existence. In Mexico in 1950, compared to costs north of the Rio Grande, life was remarkably inexpensive: one could find a good hotel for eight dollars a month, cigarettes cost six cents a pack, a quart of tequila was 40 cents, one could buy a water glass of tequila for a penny, a gallon of Cuban rum for a dollar, filet mignon was available for sixty cents a pound, a dozen oysters for thirty five cents, and encounters with young boys could be arranged for forty cents.

Burroughs' impression—and we may wonder whether it was a self-fulfilling fantasy—was that the Mexican people generally minded their own business, and this created an atmosphere of tolerance that extended to the expatriate community. His friends were not bohemian or intellectual, he advised Ginsberg in a letter of December of 1951, but former U.S. military, merchant seamen, bartenders, farmers, telephone linemen, retired policemen, and "a sprinkling of inactive criminals."

Burroughs' attitude towards Mexico began to change drastically just before the Christmas holiday of 1950 when an immigration inspector—responding to a neighbor's complaints about excessive drinking and drug use— threatened arrest and demanded a bribe. Burroughs had already begun what he called *Junk*, a narrative account of his own drug habit and the peculiarities of its demimondaine.

The idea to record his experiences, as you would in a diary, had been suggested to him by his St Louis childhood friend, Kells Elvins, with whom he had shared a house in 1938 while doing graduate work at Harvard. Elvins descended from the same social register set as Burroughs; his father was a congressman and the family had a town named after them. At Harvard, Elvins had collaborated with Burroughs on an early but paradigmatic story, "Twilight's Last Gleamings," about the sinking of the Titanic.

In the story, which was mostly written by Burroughs, the ship's captain, disguised in a woman's wig and gown, boards the first lifeboat after looting the safety deposit boxes in the purser's cabin. Throughout the story, Burroughs quoted fragments of patriotic songs like "The Star Spangled Banner" as an ironic commentary on the abuses of authority. The story was abruptly rejected by *Esquire*, causing a serious writing block that troubled Burroughs for years. Lacking confidence, he had been encouraged by Kerouac in 1944 and had been able to collaborate with him on *And the Hippos Were Boiled in Their Tanks*, but had not been able to find a subject or an authentic voice since then.

Elvins' advice—to describe what you know—made eminent sense to Burroughs. He had manifested a sable attraction to underworld activities since graduating from Harvard, a fascination with gangsters and crime that was a clear repudiation of his own class stature and background. Before he had left New York, he had created a kind of anthropological field situation by renting an apartment for Huncke on Henry Street, on the Lower East Side, happy to pay for rent and utilities as long as he was given a key and full access to the flat at any time. His purpose, the work of any novelist really, was to listen and observe in the hope of discovering a subject.

He began the *Junky* manuscript in Mexico City in the spring of 1950, dictating to a typist. The novel is an eighteenth-century form, what the French call a *roman a clef*, its key quality based on his own experience with people he knew. Using his mother's maiden name, he called his protagonist Lee. The narrative depends on a linear journey, following Burroughs' actual path from New York City to Mexico City. Its mode is traditional realism, guided by an old fashioned omniscience governing the action, and evident in the accurate description of Huncke (who is called Herman early in the novel):

> Waves of hostility and suspicion flowed out from his large brown eyes like some sort of television broadcast. The effect was almost like a physical impact. The man was small and very thin, his neck loose in the collar of his shirt. His complexion was fading from brown to mottled yellow, and pancake make-up had been heavily applied in an attempt to conceal a skin eruption. His mouth was drawn down at the corners in a grimace of petulant annoyance.

Several months later, on a subsequent visit to the Henry Street flat, Lee is met at the door by a tall, red-headed woman named Mary. The apartment looked like a Chinese restaurant with red and black lacquered tables and black curtains on the windows. The salient detail in Burroughs' description is a colored wheel "with little squares and triangles of different colors giving a mosaic effect" that had been painted on the ceiling. Burroughs may have begun his novel using the familiar model of nineteenth century narrative techniques, but the wheel he invented for his story indicates the future direction of his mosaic, kaleidoscopic architecture.

The description of Mary is another early clue to Burroughs' evolution. Moving around the room, nervously crossing and uncrossing her legs so as to reveal "a view of her anatomy in installments," Burroughs wryly observes, she tells Lee of her infatuation with a professional thief named Jack. Finally, she confesses that she suffers from a strange medical disability, that her body can no longer absorb calcium and her bones are dissolving, leading to the probable amputation of her legs and arms:

> There was something boneless about her, like a deep-sea creature. Her eyes were cold fish eyes that looked at you through a viscous medium she carried about with her. I could see those eyes in a shapeless, protoplasmic mass undulating over the dark sea floor.

Later, they snort some Benzedrine and Burroughs describes Mary as looking like a "masturbating idiot." The depiction of Mary and a number of other characters in the novel, like Subway Mike or Doolie, are clear anticipations of the phantasmagoric distortions that characterize Burroughs' subsequent development, and the natural suspicion is that this radical shift towards a post-modernist presentation was a reflection of his Mexican experience.

Burroughs completed a first draft of *Junky* by the end of 1950. He added what he called the "Mexican section" in March of 1951. *Junky* is more concerned with the intricacies of addiction than with any naturalistic representation of Mexican life. As soon as he arrives in Mexico City his search for a drug source begins. The most likely area, he advises, is one that is run-down, an ambiguous or transitional neighborhood where "dubious business enterprise touches Skid Row."

Burroughs' description of the dealer is realistic—a large straight nose, skin tight and smooth on his face, lips with a purple-blue hue "like the lips of a penis." At the same time, Burroughs evaluates with an old-fashioned narrative control that will disappear from his fiction subsequently: the dealer is "basically obscene beyond any possible vile act or practice." The portrait that ensues is composite and has a mythic dimension, and the dealer's black eyes are compared to an insect's—the first sign of a Kafkian transformative metaphor that will be more fully developed in *Naked Lunch*.

The Mexican Magnet

Junky was also affected by the tortured disintegration of his union with Joan Vollmer. Their incompatibility began with Burroughs' preference for male sexual partners, but it was compounded by their respective choice of drugs. Joan was addicted to Benzedrine, an amphetamine that quickens the pace of events, and Burroughs to morphine derivatives like heroin, which slow everything down. When Joan complained late in the summer of 1950 that Burroughs' heroin use made him boring, Burroughs slapped her in the face. Kerouac, who visited the couple at this time, would observe in *On the Road* what he called "one of the strangest" marital relationships he had seen, with a feeling he could only describe as "curiously unsympathetic and cold between them."

That fall, Joan attempted to file divorce papers, although she had become too irresolute to follow through—Mexican tequila and amphetamines had drained her. She looked haggard, her face bleary, lined and paunchy. She had gained weight and she limped, a subtle indication of how disabled she had become.

The critical factor, however, was Burroughs' infatuation with a twenty-one year old American named Lewis Marker, a very thin, gawky young man disfigured by a large birthmark below his ear, who would accompany him on the trip to Ecuador that forms the narrative center of *Queer*. Burroughs would characterize Marker as delicate and exotic in *Queer*, and it seems clear that Burroughs was very much in love with him. In a notebook, published in 2008 as *Everything Lost: The Latin American Notebook,* Burroughs reflected that he loved him "like a 4 year old child with a child's unconditional intensity."

In August, 1951, when Carr and Ginsberg visited Mexico City for the first time, Burroughs was traveling with Marker. Ginsberg saw the desperation in Joan, who seemed barely able to care for her two children. He wrote an account of being in the back of a car with Burroughs' children and Lucian and Joan in the front so drunk they could barely navigate the vehicle.

Burroughs returned just after Ginsberg's departure. Both he and Joan were depressed, baiting and goading each other. Late in the afternoon of September 7th, Burroughs brought a Star .380

automatic pistol (which he knew fired in a low trajectory) to a friend's house to sell. Burroughs, Joan, and several expatriate companions, including Lewis Marker, were drinking gin —there were four empty bottles on the floor. Known as a marksman, Burroughs was seated six feet away when Joan dramatically placed her empty glass on her head. In some versions of the story, she was said to have challenged Burroughs to shoot it off. The bullet hit her in the upper forehead.

Police were summoned, and the story was garbled in sensational newspaper headlines. Burroughs' family hired a slick attorney, a master of *mordida* named Bernabé Jurado, who managed to get Burroughs released from prison thirteen days after shooting Joan. Burroughs' exculpation was engineered by Jurado, the flamboyant Johnny Cochran of his day. The newspaper stories that ensued were full of as many glaring contradictions as the holy gospels—in one version the loaded gun was placed on the top of the refrigerator and it fired when the refrigerator door slammed. It is quite possible that Jurado knew how to plant stories so as to further obscure the truth. It is a story that might seem more plausible had the bullet penetrated a shoulder or a leg, but it entered near the hairline above her temple.

Allen Ginsberg, who saw the extent to which Joan had psychically and physically deteriorated, advanced the argument that the William Tell escapade was an instance of suicide-by-cop, that "what she most wanted was an instant out." Burroughs himself, in a letter to Ginsberg written a few years later from Tangier, speculated about the possibility of his own unconscious intent and then added the mystical, and quite unbelievable, explanation that it was "as if the brain *drew* the bullet toward it."

My strong suspicion is that Jurado persuaded key witnesses to forget what they saw, perjure themselves, or claim that Burroughs dropped the loaded gun which then misfired. Some of the witnesses had consumed prodigious quantities of alcohol and were possible drug users, making credibility an issue, as well as the brevity of the actual event itself. Released on bail, the trial dragged on for almost a year, during which Burroughs was obligated to appear before prison authorities every Monday morning at 8 a.m. When Jurado killed another man in a traffic dispute, he advised Burroughs to flee. Burroughs left the country and traveled south a week before the final verdict was issued.

A Mexican novelist named Jorge Garcia-Robles attempted to retell these events in a little book called *The Stray Bullet*; the title offers implicit support for Burroughs' argument that the shooting was accidental. The fact is, however, that both Ted Morgan and Barry Miles, Burroughs' biographers, have never been able to accurately ascertain what occurred, whose idea it was for Joan to put her drinking glass on her head, and whether the bullet was designed to hit its mark.

The longest part of Garcia-Robles' very short monograph details Burroughs' life in Mexico City and the catastrophic events leading to his shooting of Joan. His version only fogs the Burroughs myth rather than clarifying. He tends to view everything through a highly impressionistic lens, offering suppositions and recreations often based on the mistaken projections of predecessors like Ted Morgan or Barry Miles, bursts of information presented with staccato, over-simplification and sketchy summary that is less based on a genuine historical methodology than the anecdotal desire to spin a sensational story. The result is a blurred, novelistic view that leads to frequent errors of fact in a romantic style. Garcia-Robles, at one point in his narrative, refers to Burroughs as His Highness, to Ginsberg's poem "Howl" as "demonic," and to Kerouac's sidekick Neal Cassady as Dionysus.

Like D.H. Lawrence in his *Studies In Classic American Literature,* but without the intuitive talent or insight, Garcia Robles employs short phrases that are usually presented with insufficient dimension as when he claims that Kerouac "had never been weaned" from his mother. His facts are often crudely presented or just plain wrong. He alleges, for example, that Carl Solomon, who would edit *Junky,* had been Ginsberg's "former roommate at Bellevue," when in fact they met on a ward at New York State Psychiatric Hospital. Garcia-Robles tells us

Solomon had met Artaud in Paris "and so wanted to be like him that he also had electroshock therapy," but Solomon's suffering evolved along a much more complicated route than this headline suggests.

Garcia-Robles often seems to blame Burroughs for the distance and isolation that defines him, for not knowing more about Mexican literature and art, or involving himself in Mexican culture. It is an oversimplification to assert that Burroughs was dispassionate about writing, and I cannot understand what Garcia-Robles means when he argues that, for Burroughs, it was "a form of mumbling." Seduced, perhaps, by Burroughs' own ethnographic approach, Garcia-Robles makes the mistake of accepting *Junky* and a subsequent novel set in Mexico called *Queer* as a literal autobiographical record, even though Burroughs' departures from the actual occurrences are evident. The most glaring omission is any reflection in *Junky* on the shooting of Joan.

Burroughs began *Queer* in the spring of 1952 while awaiting his verdict and hosting Kerouac, who was visiting. Written after the shooting, when Burroughs was psychically stunned by the gravity of what he had done, *Queer* is a weaker novel than *Junky*. In *Queer*, Burroughs anticipates what he called his "routines"—tall stories told with a bizarrely ironic, almost vicious or aberrant edge—which perform so brilliantly autonomous a role in *Naked Lunch*.

Still, *Queer* does not quite cohere as a novel, and, like *Junky*, exists as what we might view as a laboratory text—a way of experimenting with the post-modernist techniques that would transform the possibilities for contemporary fiction in *Naked Lunch*. The "routines" are digressive and unsettling. They exist almost as rude distractions, but they fulfill Burroughs' key raconteur ability, which initially attracted Kerouac and made him predict that Burroughs would be a writer. The story he was telling, his masochistic pursuit of Marker, was not as compelling as the focused depiction of the addicted life in *Junky* and lacked its unified flow. In a sense, he was trying to restage the ingredients of *And the Hippos Were Boiled in Their Tanks*—

The Mexican Magnet

an older man obsessed with a younger one who isn't willing to reciprocate—in a more exotic South American neighborhood.

What is most surprising about *Queer*, and it is true of its predecessor *Junky* as well, is the novelist's refusal to be drawn into the exotic, to attend to the recognizable local color characteristics of Mexico City or Latin American life in the early 1950s. In fact, what he omits, deliberately it would seem, he highlights at the beginning of his 1985 introduction to the novel:

> The City appealed to me. The slum areas compared favorably with anything in Asia for sheer filth and poverty. People would shit all over the street, then lie down and sleep in it with the flies crawling in and out of their mouths. Entrepreneurs, not infrequently lepers, built fires on street corners and cooked up hideous, stinking, nameless messes of food, which they dispensed to passersby. Drunks slept right on the sidewalks of the main drag, and no cops bothered them.

In *Junky*, Burroughs argued that most travel books failed to represent what was important to him: the salient political conditions governing human behavior. So he tends to omit the visceral details that a writer like Kerouac would systematically register. *Queer* was only published thirty-three years after Burroughs wrote it, a history that might suggest it was practically an abortive attempt. At the end of the novel, Burroughs includes a dream of returning to Mexico City which he characterizes as a "terminal of space-time travel, a waiting room where you grab a quick drink while you wait for your train." The image of the transitional anonymity of the waiting room reflects Burroughs' use of Mexico in his fiction, but it also suggests a writer who had been so traumatized by his own action—shooting Joan—that he was prepared only to occupy a recess so interior that outside events and conditions became minimized.

At the beginning of *Queer*, Burroughs remembered that "a

silence peculiar to Mexico seeped into the room, a vibrating, soundless hum." The silence occupies his protagonist's body, whose face is described as going "slack and blank. The effect was curiously spectral, as though you could see through his face." The effect of Mexico and the unspecified, implicit terrors of an alien culture envelop *Queer* with an almost sentient, mystical vibration or hum. Analogous in effect to the miasma around Roderick Usher's mansion, this "vibrating soundless hum" is the register of Mexico on Burroughs which had to be deeply associated with the shooting he always claimed was both accidental and determined by a haunting, occupying, malevolent force he called the "ugly spirit."

The most extraordinary aspect of *Queer* is the commentary Burroughs contributed to the 1985 edition. When he began his piece, he acknowledged that he was "paralyzed with a heavy reluctance, a writer's block like a straitjacket" because the poison of his past was still threatening and seemed too difficult to remember. *Queer*, he wrote in 1985, "was motivated and formed by an event which is never mentioned, in fact is carefully avoided: the accidental shooting death of my wife, Joan, in September, 1951" and "I am forced to the appalling conclusion that I would never have become a writer but for Joan's death."

The claim may be considered hyperbolic since he had already written most of *Junky* prior to the shooting. *Junky*—the publishers felt that *Junk*, Burroughs' proposed title, made the book sound as if its subject were garbage—is a linear narrative account of Burroughs' southward migration from Manhattan, to Texas, to New Orleans, and then to Mexico. He continued to alter and add to the manuscript through the summer of 1952 when it was accepted by A.A. Wyn, a mediocre publisher of detective novels that were more apt to be found in drug stores than bookstores.

Unlike most travel writing "which never gives the information I want," Burroughs observed in *Junky*, the real territorial objective of the novel is the landscape of the drug culture, the "invisible mouth" that influenced Burroughs' worldview. Written, as Oliver Harris has noted, in his cogent introduction to the fiftieth anniversary edition, almost like an "ethnographic field report," Burroughs describes his sensational subject from a calm ordered clinician's perspective, very differently from Nelson Algren's National Book winning bestseller of 1950, *The Man With the Golden Arm.*

The topography and actual culture of Mexico seem tangential or even incidental as far as Burroughs' deeper purposes. "In Mexico, your wishes have a dream power," he states in the novel. The quality of dream as drugged nightmare informs his novel in a contrapuntal dance with the more factual, sociological observations on the conditions of addiction. When he reaches Mexico, in the last section of *Junky,* it seems more sinisterly dangerous for the American *gringo* than any place north of the border, with the threat of violence or corruption more Kafkaesque, normative, acceptable, and expected.

One scene, set in a cantina he names Lola's, seems characteristic of the sort of fear he would later magnify as he did with the Mayan and Aztec torture rituals in *Naked Lunch.* Burroughs is reading a newspaper when he overhears someone talking about lobotomy. At another table, two young men are flirting with two giggling Mexican girls. Burroughs situates them in Samuel Beckett's hell:

> The conversations had a nightmare flatness, talking dice spilled in the tube metal chairs, human aggregates disintegrating in cosmic inanity, random events in a dying universe where everything is exactly what it appears to be, and no other relation than juxtaposition is possible.

The "talking dice" image suggests the absurd science fiction imagery of Burroughs' masterpiece, *Naked Lunch.* The omniscient perspective of *Junky* is always informative, unlike the kaleidoscopic and fluidly discontinuous fragmentation that would inform the more cinematic presentation *of Naked Lunch.* In *Junky,* for example, Burroughs offers a history of a three hundred pound junk merchant named Lupita who "pays off to operate wide open, like she was running a grocery store," and ultimately monopolizes the heroin market with an inferior product.

Near the beginning of *Naked Lunch*, Lupita reappears in a fragment, as an inexplicable, totemistic, ceremonial figure; a warning as Burroughs, driven by an unidentified female, approaches Mexico City "where Lupita sits like an Aztec earth goddess doling out her little papers of lousy shit." The line duplicates what Burroughs had written about Lupita in *Junky*, where it is presented as part of an old-fashioned omniscient portrait explaining how she was able to control the narcotics trade in Mexico City. In *Naked Lunch*, however, the repeated line is like the view of Mexico that is filtered through the novel. Lupita now flashes by the reader without the comfort of any explanations in a mysteriously jarring appearance. Her name, with its lupine connotations, is elliptical, an ominously menacing reflection of Burroughs' changing view of Mexico.

III. Beyond Darwin's Chain

"I know you will enjoy Mexico, since you can really relax here and save money," Burroughs wrote to Kerouac in March, 1950. Burroughs believed, erroneously, that Kerouac would have money to spend and to save because of royalties from his first novel.

An aspiring novelist, Kerouac's origins were lower working class. He had been raised in Lowell, Massachusetts, a mill town that provided poorly paid jobs for immigrants; the Merrimack River flowing through it afforded cheap electric power. Living in a French-Canadian ghetto, as a child, Kerouac spoke a Creole called *joual*, a spoken, rather than a written dialect. His father had a small print shop, destroyed when the Merrimac River flooded its banks at the height of the Depression in 1936. Kerouac played football in high school and was able to attend Columbia University on an athletic scholarship.

The Mexican Magnet

Kerouac's athletic scholarship was abruptly discontinued when he refused to continue playing football after an injury. Instead, patriotically in wartime, he shipped out on six dangerous merchant marine bomb runs, transporting munitions to the European theater during the war.

At Columbia Kerouac had set a record for cutting classes because he stayed up all night listening to a new jazz sound that would profoundly influence his own sense of the possibilities of rhythm in prose. Minton's, a club in Harlem, a mile East of Columbia University, had opened its stage to a group of African-American musicians—Dizzy Gillespie, Charley Parker, Lester Young, Thelonius Monk—who responded to the set pieces and careful arrangements, the harmonic dance-inspired swing of the preceding era, with a dissonantly, jagged, angry, agitated, and extremely improvised series of sounds they called Bop.

A white anomaly in the room, Kerouac was drawn to this group and befriended by Lester Young who brought him to jam sessions when Minton's closed, and passed him his first funny looking marijuana cigarette in a cab one night. It may have been Kerouac's first taste of a marginal, extralegal, outsider experience, his first entry into a hipster world.

A more serious brush with criminality occurred immediately after Lucien Carr's murder of David Kammerer. Early on the morning after the murder, Carr woke Burroughs and told him what had happened. Burroughs' advice was for Carr to get a lawyer and report what had occurred to the authorities. Dissatisfied with that advice, Carr woke Kerouac who accompanied him on a long walk to the Museum of Modern Art, stopping at a few bars that were open that early for another drink. The next morning, Kerouac was arrested as a material witness.

Kerouac's parents, living in Ozone Park, Queens, were scandalized by this compromising of family honor. Kerouac was briefly jailed until his girlfriend's lawyer allowed her to put up the money for bail with the proviso that the couple would marry. The marriage was the first of three for Kerouac, only lasting a few months.

In 1946, after Burroughs and Joan Vollmer left the apartment on 115th Street for their Texas farm, Kerouac lived with his parents in Ozone Park. He signed on with the merchant marine but did not appear for another maritime voyage because his father developed cancer of the spleen. That ship was hit by a German torpedo and sank in the Atlantic. While his mother continued to work in shoe factories, Kerouac cared for his father. While he did—in his parent's cramped, tiny, three room apartment—he completed his first novel, *The Town and the City*, a sprawling, traditional *Bildungsroman* based on his Lowell childhood. It was an apprentice work, but good enough to be published by Harcourt, Brace in early spring of 1950.

Though the novel's publication was certainly confirmation of his talents, its mixed reception and poor sales were discouraging. His novel had been quickly forgotten, he complained in a letter, and he was afflicted with "the curse of Melville." He was struggling to find a new form for a novel based on a series of road trips he had taken with a new friend named Neal Cassady, a wild firebrand carouser who fascinated him. Partly raised by an alcoholic father on the Denver bowery, spending time in hobo encampments as a child and in reform school afterwards, Cassady was another marginal outsider, a questionable influence like Huncke.

That summer, Kerouac was driven to Mexico City by Cassady, who was seeking to take advantage of Mexican law to divorce his wife Carolyn. While visiting Joan and Burroughs, Kerouac developed a severe case of dysentery. They nursed him back to health on a curious diet of daily quantities of marijuana and some morphine. Recovered, Kerouac was as intoxicated by wandering the streets of Mexico City, a *flâneur* in a region he somehow connected to the fraternal camaraderie of the immigrant communities of his Lowell childhood. Returning by train to Laredo, Texas, he crossed the border in August "with a kilo of cured shit round waist in a silk scarf" as he confessed in his journal, *Windblown World*. The "shit" was slang code for marijuana, properly aged, and the diary entry itself an admission of how profoundly the experience of Mexico had affected him.

Always more romantic and rhapsodic than the more cynical

The Mexican Magnet

Burroughs, Kerouac's idealizations of Mexican life irritated Burroughs. Five months before shooting Joan, Burroughs reacted harshly in a letter written in May of 1951 toward Kerouac's comparison of Mexico to his Lowell childhood:

> Mexico is not simple or gay or idyllic. It is nothing like a French Canadian naborhood (sic). It is an Oriental country that reflects 2000 years of disease and poverty and degradation and stupidity and slavery and brutality and psychic and physical terrorism. Mexico is sinister and gloomy and chaotic with the special chaos of a dream. I like it myself, but it isn't everybody's taste.

Kerouac believed that one of his eighteenth century Breton ancestors had settled in Quebec with a Mohawk wife, so he was particularly willing to identify with indigenous cultures. One reason for Kerouac's attraction to Mexico was the vitality and color of what he called the Mexican fellaheen, the surviving remnants of the pre-Columbian cultures that descended from the Mayan and Aztec empires. In an undated sequence in his journal, *Windblown World*, he called "A Tarahumare Afternoon," he admired what he imagined as a pastoral idyll:

> I go across sad railroad plazas of dust to Juarez Bridge and cross for two cents into the blissful peace of the Fellaheen village at hot sun noon— smells of tortilla, drowse of children & dogs, heat, little long streets—I go clear out of town to river levee and squat on ground and see on this side an Indian mother kneeling at the river washing clothes with little baby son clinging lovingly to her back—Thought, "If my mother was only simple as to do her wash at the river."
> —Felt happiness.

Another consequence of his early Mexican sojourns may have been, at least in part, the break through scroll manuscript of *On the Road*, which was composed in April of 1951, based on the episodic adventures Kerouac and Cassady shared while discovering the expanse of the United States. Written in less than a month, with Kerouac typing up to twenty hours a day, staying awake with coffee laced with Benzedrine, the publication of the novel was stymied for six long years, a cause for considerable consternation and depression for Kerouac.

In the spring of 1952, Kerouac returned to Mexico again, to visit Burroughs in Mexico City—"a mad genius in littered rooms." *Junky* was awaiting publication, while Burroughs was writing *Queer* and attending his trial for the shooting of Joan. Kerouac was working on an extension of *On the Road* called *Visions of Cody* as well as *Dr. Sax*, a story based on his Lowell childhood. The apartment was too small for two writers, so Kerouac often had to work in a small hallway bathroom. Because of the trial and the difficulties Burroughs was having with his own manuscript, Burroughs was irascible and Kerouac's lack of money did not help alleviate the tension.

In a long letter to Ginsberg, written on May 10th 1952, Kerouac described his trip from California to Mexico City. Neal Cassady, with his wife Carolyn and their babies "all gypsied and happy," had deposited him at the Mexican border. In Sonora, Arizona, he purchased a second-class bus ticket on a high, narrow bus with wooden benches, singing children and goats on its roof that stopped in Culiacán, which he called the opium center of the world:

> I ate tortillas and carne in African stick huts in the jungle with pigs rubbing against my legs; I drank pure pulque from a pail, fresh from the field, from the plant, unfermented, pure milk of pulque makes you get the giggles, is the greatest drink in the world. I ate strange new fruit, erenos, mangoes, all kinds. In the back of the bus, drinking mescal, I sang bop for the Mexican

singers who were curious to hear what it sounded like . . .

Smoking joints laced with opium, he was celebrating, exultant, "beyond Darwin's chain." Later in the letter, he reminds Ginsberg that his genealogy is partly Indian, and that with his French-Canadian mind he can understand everything his new Indian companions say, "digging everything, all of it, almost perfectly," even when one of them declares in Spanish that "the earth is an Indian thing"—a line he would transpose with a sacramental insistence to *On the Road*.

Kerouac returned to Mexico in 1955 and 1956, living in a rooftop stone hovel and working on *Tristessa*, a novel about a tortured love affair he had with a Mexican junkie prostitute named Esperanza Villanueva. The relationship was particularly dangerous because Esperanza was also sleeping with the police chief of Mexico City who could order assassinations with impunity. Practically living as a vagrant on pennies a day, he was torn by the despair he felt at the inability to get *On the Road* published. Trying to resolve his depression with an intense exploration of Buddhism, he was then more fully prepared to describe the poverty of Mexico.

This included aspects of urban Mexico like Tristessa's tenement shack with the rain stained pornography on the kitchen walls, with the rooster, chickens, and dove pecking at garbage in the kitchen—the kind of authentic detail that Burroughs seems to have ignored. In the streets outside, a phantasmagoria lit by candles, dim bulbs, and lanterns, Kerouac walks "with one quick Walt Whitman look," past the hundreds of whores with crooking fingers on Panama Street, over giant mud puddles and five foot ditches, past a half a mile of food stands "devouring whole mouthloads of fire."

The joyous discovery that animates Kerouac's view of Mexico is the energy that fuels his driven rhythms, the reason Sal Paradise finds the backbreaking labor of picking cotton with his Mexican lover Terry in *On the Road* so glorious, or the African-American Denver ghetto so harmonious a community. Dean and

Sal, Kerouac's feckless protagonists, finally reach a town called Sabinas Hidalgo in Mexico near the end of On *the Road*.

Dean, the yea-sayer, speculates that its inhabitants are without suspicion, soft, and subdued: "the people here are straight and kind and don't put down any bull." The undeveloped frontier bustle of the town has its appeal:

> The main street was muddy and full of holes. On each side were dirty broken-down adobe fronts. Burros walked in the streets with packs. Barefoot women watched us from dark doorways. The street was crowded with people on foot . . .

Even the subsequent, sordid disorder of the culminating Mexican brothel scene cannot cancel Kerouac's love for Mexico. As he had declared earlier in the novel, when picking cotton with his Mexican lover, Terry, the landowners who hired him "thought I was Mexican, of course, and in a way I am." This empathy, and the romantic emphasis that reinforces it, determines his view. It seems quite deliberately innocent, not mindlessly myopic as the more mean spirited Burroughs might have seen it, almost an unconscious spiritual counter to a profoundly debilitating despair and guilt that afflicted him, and that he battled with Buddhism in the 1950s and booze until his early death in 1969.

IV. Into the Volcano

Allen Ginsberg was twelve years younger than Burroughs, and four years younger than Kerouac. Raised in Paterson, New Jersey, a working class community, his father taught English for forty years at Paterson High School and wrote very conventional, metrically arranged poems. His mother's history of mental instability, breakdown, and eventual institutional lobotomy cauterized Ginsberg's early years, and those of his older brother,

The Mexican Magnet

Eugene.

Ginsberg took a while to graduate from Columbia because he kept getting into trouble. The most distressing occasion was an instance of fickle outrage. He inscribed with his finger on the dirty film of his window two lines of early graffiti: "Fuck the Jews!" and "Butler has no balls." The Dean of Students to whom this was reported was unconcerned with the first observation—Columbia used quotas and had not welcomed Jews until quite recently. However, Nicholas Murray Butler had once been Columbia's longtime president and so, adding the derogatory reference resulted in Ginsberg's suspension. During that period, he also studied at the Merchant Marine Academy in Brooklyn and earned seaman's papers.

The second occasion of bad behavior occurred two years after finally graduating from Columbia. It almost landed him in jail and certainly sent him to the madhouse, the route his mother had taken. One day in early February, 1949, his old friend Herbert Huncke knocked at his door in a delirious and suicidal state. His feet were bruised, bloody, and sore; his skin was blistered and festering. Even though Ginsberg had not seen his friend for some time, he could not turn him away when he was in such distress, and he allowed Huncke to move into his apartment. Soon, Huncke's friends, Little Jack Melody, a small-time thief (who figures as Jack in *Junky*), and his girlfriend, a tall, redheaded beauty named Priscilla Armiger (the boneless Mary in *Junky*) began to haunt the apartment. After Huncke recuperated, Ginsberg fell ill. When he recovered, he noticed that the apartment was filled with contraband material—stolen suits, coats in a closet, audio equipment. When he realized it had been stolen, he demanded that Huncke leave and take everything with him.

Little Jack appeared with a car to bring the stolen goods to Queens. Ginsberg's mistake was to take advantage of the ride to drop off some papers at his brother's home. There was an accident on Northern Boulevard and Little Jack, with honed criminal instincts, fled the scene, but Ginsberg's papers were found in the car. Now he was an accessory to a felony. Even though his sense of respectability was tested, one of his Columbia mentors, the critic Lionel Trilling, pleaded with the District Attorney not to try him. A loyal Columbia alumnus, Frank Hogan, allowed Ginsberg to be admitted to Columbia Psychiatric Hospital, probably the best mental facility in the city, at that time. He spent almost a year there and met Carl Solomon, who would be the dedicatee of his poem "Howl" and the editor of *Junky*.

For many years after his release from Columbia Psychiatric, Ginsberg felt trapped in stasis in an emotional dead-end. He was ambivalent about his homosexual desires that he related to an inability to discover his own individual voice as a poet, perhaps despite the brilliance of his undergraduate imitations of sixteenth and seventeenth century poetry.

When Kerouac's first novel was published in 1950, unhappy that his poems were not getting published, Ginsberg returned to his hometown of Paterson, New Jersey. Encouraged by Kerouac, he began an informal tutorial in the virtues of natural speech and a less self-consciously literary diction with an older poet, William Carlos Williams, who practiced pediatrics in Paterson. This friendship became a turning point for him.

In December, 1953, Ginsberg hitchhiked south to Florida, visiting Burroughs' former lover Lewis Marker in Jacksonville and Burroughs' parents in Palm Beach. Then he took a plane to Havana, and another to Yucatán. He would spend the next six months in Mexico. Kerouac (drawing on D.H. Lawrence's concept) had informed Ginsberg that he was going to a place where he could find himself in an encircling timelessness. Though this could lead to potential terrors, it could also become a route to freedom from one's conditioned expectations.

He experienced a glimmer of such freedom at the eleventh century pyramid ruins of Chichén Itzá:

> Stars over pyramids—tropic night, forest of chirruping insects . . . great stone . . . relief of unknown perceptions, half a thousand years old—and earlier in day saw stone cocks a thousand years old grown over with moss and

batshit dripping in vaulted room of stone stuck in the wall.

While there were frustrations for Ginsberg, caused both by his lack of money and fluency in Spanish, there were some gratifying encounters, particularly one in which he was invited to participate in a New Year's celebration in Mérida and, wandering into a bar for tequila a few days later, met the "brilliant Spaniard," as he eulogized him in "Howl," "to talk about America and Eternity."

From Mérida, Ginsberg traveled by train and bus to Chiapas, in the extreme south of Mexico, part of the Mayan region that the Mexicans had seized from Guatemala, its smaller neighbor to its south, after the United States defeated them in the Mexican War and annexed the southwest. At the edge of an inaccessible forest jungle, the temple ruins of Palenque had been smothered by trees and impenetrable vines, invisible for over a thousand years, reclaimed as it were by nature. Camping at the ruins in Palenque, he was stunned by the archaic resonance he felt in the seventh century remnants of Mayan civilization, which for him emphasized the transience of human existence. While living in an archeologists' camp, he met Karena Shields, an amateur archeologist. When Ginsberg complained that he was quickly running out of money, she generously invited him to stay at her cocoa plantation, and she proved to be an able exponent of Mayan history, symbolism, and metaphysics. Playfully, he called her his "white goddess."

He was living communally on tortillas and *frijole*s, he wrote to Kerouac on February 14, 1954. Tasting fried grasshoppers and roasted monkey, sleeping in a hammock under a thatched roof on an open platform without side walls, Ginsberg felt liberated— he was playing drums several hours daily on ceiba logs in the Mayan fashion. Early in the morning, or late in the afternoon when the sun was descending, he would work in the banana or cocoa groves, cutting, washing, fermenting, and drying the cocoa. Shields' *finca* was practically in the jungle, which added to the exoticism and uninhibited freedom Ginsberg experienced there. At midday, he would walk naked, ankle, waist, or neck deep up a rocky clear stream, lush with plantains, lianas, and giant mahogany trees filled with monkeys.

Ginsberg was entering a new spaciousness not often available to young men raised in a suburban, middle class setting. This is the cosmic kind of loafing indolence of which Whitman was accused, and this is reflected in the second stanza of the poem Ginsberg was writing while at the *finca*, dedicated to Karena Shields:

> — One could pass valuable months
> and years perhaps a lifetime
> doing nothing but lying in a hammock
> reading prose with the white doves
>   copulating underneath
> and monkeys barking in the interior
>   of the mountain
> and I have succumbed to this temptation—

Although the form of "Siesta in Xbalba" still showed the formal influence of his mentor, William Carlos Williams' triadic meter, variable foot, and short line, the long poem also revealed a breakthrough in consciousness for Ginsberg. Conflating what he had seen at Chichén Itzá, Uxmal, and Palenque with the mummified corpses in the catacombs that he had seen at Guanajuato, Ginsberg seemed to be intent on deciphering the "hieroglyphs of Eternity," while preparing for a crucial moment when ego could disappear, or at least diminish:

>   my soul might shatter
> at one primal moment's
>   sensation of the vast
> movement of divinity.

Near the end of his stay at Karena Shields' *finca*, Ginsberg felt earthquake tremors and heard rumors of disappearing villages. He was able to reach Yajalón, a small town surrounded

The Mexican Magnet

by mountains, near the reputed epicenter, partly by getting a ride in a small 1914 biplane (which crashed several weeks later) and partly by mule. Joining an expedition of local tribesmen to determine whether there had been a volcanic fissure on the top of Mount Acavalna, he was again plunged into an authentic Mexico with bamboo drums in a church at night, women lighting candles in front of an altar decorated with old, German religious paintings, and dolls representing bearded, black Indian figures with Jesus, when, after an explosive boom, the entire mountain began to shake.

The next day he accompanied another group of white robed Indians from a neighboring village who wanted to see whether a sacred cave on the other side of the mountain had been sealed by the quake. As Ginsberg entered its "stupendous" mouth, he saw that part of the cave ceiling had collapsed and huge rocks, rubble, and trees lay scattered. There were several more booms and trembles. The cave was open, he wrote Kerouac on April 4, 1954, "like some awful dream vision, that big you know—and full of pulpit formations, and naves and arches, like a Piranesi drawing don't you know, pilasters and arks and giant dark religious formations."

In a region where the indigenous population did not speak Spanish, but instead the Mayan language, *Tzeltal*, Ginsberg was introduced to a part of Mexico that did seem "beyond Darwin's chain" as Kerouac had promised. The effect was transformative. A little over a year later he would compose "Howl," a poem that would alter the direction of American poetry and become the first clarion call of the Beat Generation.

V. Impact

Burroughs, the glacial iceberg of the Beat group, could seem unaffected by what he called in a moment of characteristically political incorrectness the "oriental" quality of Mexico, with the drunks sleeping soundly on streets where lepers prepared and sold food. The sinister "vibrating soundless hum" he imagined and equated with Mexico was the metaphor he invented for a sense of evil catastrophe that haunted him. That hum was an isolating factor, an invisible wall that inevitably separated him from his surroundings, preventing him from any identification that was not ironic. Whether it was the drugs he was using or the absurdity he felt in daily Mexican life, or more probably a combination of the two, the experience was enough to rupture a recurrent writing block, to trigger the composition of his first two novels, and to leave an indelible imprint on *Naked Lunch*.

Usually free of irony, Kerouac in Mexico comes closest to connecting with what he called "wailing humanity," seeing its poverty and consequent disease compassionately. Like some Whitman in lower Manhattan a century earlier, he existed in willful denial of his own enormous vulnerability as the *gringo* from a culture than had swallowed half of Mexico before the middle of the nineteenth century. Instead, he projects a state of immunity, freedom, and fraternity, an ecstatic camaraderie reaching out to those who cannot understand his language or the bop songs he sings in the bus outside Culiacán. The result is the kind of transport characteristically associated with Kerouac.

"Something that you feel will find its own form" Kerouac predicted in his "List of Essentials." The new direction this precept suggested represented a new direction for American writing in the 1950s. Kerouac's Mexican journeys, particularly as imagined in *Tristessa*, became a trigger for that release of feeling, a counter for a historical period marked by apathy and conformity, and a literature dominated by the restraint of T.S. Eliot's "escape from personality" credo.

At the same time, the attraction of Mexico for both Burroughs and Kerouac could have been its pervasive poverty, its radical difference from American affluence. Bonnie Bremser spoke about this in an interview with Nancy Grace in a valuable collection called *Breaking the Rule of Cool*: "It was almost as though the people in Mexico are so open to their poverty, or so open to the oppression of being downtrodden . . . That's what was identifying with, that darkness in myself as, okay, now the worst has happened to me, yet these people can accept me."

However, of the three writers under consideration here, Ginsberg may have been the most affected by Mexico, perhaps because in the southern and unchanged parts of Chiapas he could experience an even more profound sense of the "encircling timelessness" Kerouac promised. As he deciphered what he called the "hieroglyphs of Eternity" around him, and measured signs of the transience of human effort, he began to understand how his own pronounced sense of ego could interfere with the flow that could result in poetry. Mexico was seminal for him and "Howl" became his immediate horizon.

VI. Epilogue: A Plunge to the South

The Mexican novelist Garcia-Robles accused Burroughs of shutting himself off from the culture of Mexico, inhabiting a void of his own preferentiality. While it is true that Burroughs avoided the more profuse naturalistic details provided by Kerouac in *Tristessa,* it is also possible to understand that his probing of the Latin experience may have occurred on a more profoundly felt emotional level.

Cool and distant, as remote as he often was, the crucible of the murder of Joan, and the further disjunction of his attorney Jurado's advice to flee before the court issued its verdict, must have throttled Burroughs. He precipitously left Mexico in December of 1952, selling some of his possessions to a waiter in a Chinese restaurant and giving the rest away to an ice cream vendor. Kerouac, remaining in Mexico City at the time, poignantly remembered that Burroughs seemed thin, forlorn, tragic in his moldy room: "Burroughs is gone at last—3 years in Mexico—lost everything, his children, his patrimony—all lost....Bill hurries off into the night solitaire—ah soul—throwing in his bag, at last, picture of Lucien and Allen—."

Burroughs began a seven month journey to Columbia, Ecuador, and Peru in search of ayahuasca—yagé for short—a jungle vine prepared by a tribal shaman so powerful that it was reputed to induce telepathic states. His Harvard classmate, Richard Evans Schultes, had recently returned from more than a decade on foot and paddling in canoes in the Amazon basin, where he had learned about ayahuasca, warned of the extinction of over ninety tribal groups, and the eventual destruction of the Amazon rainforest by developers.

Burroughs had less planetary concerns. At this point in his life, he was fascinated by the possibility of inducing telepathic states. Such a condition held considerable appeal for a writer who so often provoked a subliminal magic in sense or sound, though it might have equal appeal for a religious leader or a politician for that matter. My view is that, for Burroughs, at least initially, yagé represented a route of possible exorcism. Drugs derived from opium tend to envelop the subject in a comforting balm, a protective cloud, but the yagé concoction is more intense, searing, and dislocating than the most potent psychedelics.

By bus, truck, and canoe, Burroughs travelled from Bogota to the deep interior region on the Putumayo River. In town after town, he was obligated to register with police. His progress was interrupted by constant police checks and harassment because of guerrilla revolutionary activities. He wrote Ginsberg that he had a gun buried in his bags under his medicines. The police looked like "the end result of atomic radiation." They slouched on street corners with evident hostility, "waiting to shoot somebody."

It could not have helped matters that Burroughs was using a camera as a sort of notebook, even though he felt some ambivalence about photographing. Despite the validity of his papers, Burroughs was arrested in the town of Puerto Assis, a desolate place with one muddy street, a rundown hotel, a few shops, and a Capuchin mission. After five days, he was escorted by police to another town and jailed for a night. He was suddenly released the following morning without explanation. It was another instance in a pattern without logic or reason that by now he expected south of the Rio Grande, and it would leave its imprint on everything he wrote subsequently, beginning with *Naked Lunch*.

The inauspicious beginning of his journey was followed by a series of absurd encounters and incongruities. Frequently, Burroughs was bullied by nondescript customs inspectors, only to be regarded as a dignitary because of an unfounded rumor that he was the secret representative of an oil company.

In a letter to Ginsberg, he described the town of Puerto Leguízamo as an illustration of the omnipresent Conradian miasma:

> The place looks like it was left over from a receding flood. Rusty abandoned machinery scattered here and there. Swamps in the middle of town. Unlighted streets you can sink up to your knees in. There are five whores in town sitting out in front of blue walled cantinas. Young kids cluster around the whores with the immobile concentration of tom cats. The whores sit there in the muggy night under one naked electric bulb in the blare of juke box music, waiting.

Burroughs saw disease everywhere, leprosy, and advanced tuberculosis, beggars with withered hands: "It seemed like every second person had a harelip or one leg shorter than the other or a blind festering eye." He succeeded in finding several Indian shamans in Columbia and then in Peru who prepared and administered the yagé vine, an intense hallucinatory experience which surely left its impact on *Naked Lunch*.

The *curanderos'* administration of yagé had not exorcised or cured him, and in May he wrote to Ginsberg that he was suffering from "a horrible sick feeling of final desolation." This dejection got worse as summer wore on. As Oliver Harris has explained in his introduction to *Everything Lost: The Latin American Notebook,* Burroughs' scrawled entries reveal a man in chaotic circumstances, caught in his own despair and contemplating disaster. Burroughs' Spenglerian awareness "of looming cultural catastrophe," as Harris puts it, "is grounded in his own private crisis." This crisis, of course, is the personal consequence, the guilt, and horror of having destroyed whatever semblance of family existed for him when he shot his wife.

In July and August of 1953, in a square, plain school notebook with cheap lined paper and a black cover, Burroughs began to juxtapose his reflections, notes on his travels, fiction sketches, dreams of Marker, with a circling repetition, all blurred, fragmented, often cryptic, and sometimes elliptical to the point of enigma. The question that inevitably occurs is whether the pain was too intense for the clarity of *Junky* or *Queer*? What is key is that the method he was discovering—however disordered by drugs and emotional deprivation—anticipates the postmodernist swirl he would later invent for *Naked Lunch*.

Parts of *Everything Lost* flash back to Burroughs' final search in Mexico for Lewis Marker, his unreciprocating former lover. "The pain inside," he writes, was "sharp and definite as a physical wound." When he learned Marker has left Mexico with a handsome older man, "a wave of misery and pain hit [him] like a main line shot, settling in the lungs and around the heart." Now Mexico seemed like a waiting room in a train station after all the trains had left or no longer stopped. Later, he admitted he had fled the "gruesome cultural straight jacket" of the United States only to come to detest Mexico. He dreamed of an atomic cloud, its purple black shadow emanating from Chile, and viewed his travel as a "disaster that lost [him] everything [he] had of value."

Near the end of *Everything Lost,* he states that the Indians are deprived, "sad and beaten," like "fish caught in a shrinking pond." Somewhat like Kurtz at the end of Conrad's *Heart of Darkness*, language begins to break down on the verge of imminent collapse. His language becomes even more fragmented, devolving into broken disconnected shards. Practically, his penultimate words are "The giving up. The quitting. The Resignation."

He is so outside the strata of normative existence that he can see what he has left. The problem is control, he speculates, "growing like a cancer, a proliferating tumor of stupidity." Two years later, in Tangier, he would accept this concept as the central metaphor in *Naked Lunch*. His experiences in Mexico and South America had prepared, and liberated, him to write his masterpiece.

II
The Oaxaca Letters

Sunday night,
10/13/74

Dear Mellon,

Several hours of sadness on the plane seated next to a young man from Mexico City who spoke no English. He slept through most of the flight in his shades. Isolation—a twig plunged into the turbulent Mississippi—so sorry that I couldn't have departed on a more celebratory note, disappointed and so confused over my place in your future. All this compounded by the paradox of wanting you to accompany me, while knowing you feel suffocated in my orbit, and the lonely realization that I need solitude to read and write.

Our lives will now spin in different directions, more exciting, perhaps, than the sordid mediocrities of money worries—the terrible trap we felt the night before my departure. I should not feel so guilty since you want to free yourself, which may be a necessary step for each of us, but the dull pain I feel at the edge of my nerves is the result of the sundering, the severance, the dissolution of a nine year bond. On the plane, I read the first page of a slim Mexican travel journal by Lawrence Ferlinghetti—lines that so apply to me now: "My soul in various pieces and I attempting to reassemble it, mistaking bird cries for ecstatic song when they are really cries of despair."

By the time we reached Mexico City, my head was in a better place. There was no room in the hotel your friend Eleanor Fields recommended. Like some fool, I lugged my baggage for blocks—burdened, desolate, downtrodden. Suddenly, a travel guide appeared trying to sell me a tour. I got him to recommend a place, and he drove me to the Alameda, a fifteen-minute walk from the Zona Rosa, the hip section Eleanor told us about. I was settled by mid-afternoon.

By late afternoon I wandered into the Museum de Beaux Arts and admired the Tamayo, Diego Rivera, and Orozco murals—communistic cartoons—one labeling a skull "Eternidad"—but often powerful in a grand manner like Goya. Then I walked to the Zona Rosa and spent four hours promenading, window gazing with the tourists. It is a bit like our Greenwich Village, except young Mexican girls parade in pairs and trios and seem very prim despite short skirts and tight pants. The boys seem timid, many couples holding hands, embracing, the men *muy romantico*.

Walked so long I got lost in the labyrinth of the unfamiliar and needed a taxi to find my hotel.

Love,
John

The Oaxaca Letters

10/14/74

Dear Mellon,

Walked to 212 Orizaba where William Burroughs lived after the catastrophic shooting of his wife, Joan Vollmer, where Kerouac later visited and, cramped for space, wrote *Doctor Sax* in the hall bathroom. Approached by two young men who asked whether I wanted to score. On the Metro—marble floors, beautiful, silent, crowded but clean trains—to the suburb of Xolo: ramshackle dwellings, tin huts squeezed together, many stray dogs, hundreds of kids playing with tires and tin cans in the streets, but no luck.

Mexico City laid out in circles like Paris: noisy streets and too many cars; air quality inferior even on Sunday. Small parks and fountains. Architecturally, an amalgam of Colonial Spanish style villas and new apartment complexes. Narrow streets with smells of chili and bad sewage from one step to the next. In spots, city reminds me of Venice with its curving alleys. Spent afternoon in a small park near my hotel. Approached by a procession of doleful shoeshine boys. One of them was shoeless. Clowns performing to gleeful audiences. People here seem startled or amused by my long hair and beard. Children point and their mothers laugh.

I feel no paranoia, even though I don't know the language. I can make some single word requests, and I've gotten on a few bus rides (10 cents). Visited two Catholic churches and listened to services to hear accents. Called Eleanor's friend Jorge, but no one was there.

Love,
John

10/15/74

Dear Mellon,

Visited American Express this morning and wrote a $300 personal check. Then I took a long, crowded bus ride to the University of Mexico—a huge campus with modern buildings all decorated with colorful murals. Tried to find the English Department and got someone to draw me a map, but it seemed like miles of uncertainty. Somehow found a center for foreign students, and was told that classes in English were held on the third floor. Sat in on a class in Uruguayan history. Small class with an American instructor. He told me he had been teaching at this "dead end job" for six years.

 Resumed wandering around the sprawling campus and met an Englishwoman named Mary who accompanied me. She is trying to find a teaching position. After an hour, with no success in reaching an English Department, we took the bus back to Zona Rosa. Rollercoaster ride with an anarchic bus driver, speaking to pals in the street, playing a radio at a very high volume. Mary is supporting herself as an *au pair*. She told me the train to Oaxaca only costs $5, but flying is $25. I'll take the bus tomorrow, and I'll write when I get there.

          Love,
          John

p.s. Last night, before sleeping, read the beginning of Bonnie Bremser's *For Love of Ray*, a somewhat harrowing account of her flight to Mexico with Kerouac's pal, Ray Bremser, and their infant daughter, Rachel. Her initial impression of the central bus station in Mexico City is a "swelter" of disreputable looking people who appear homeless. It seems like the reaction of someone who is afraid. In Veracruz, Bonnie and Ray rent a little yellow stucco house with inner walls of the same stucco and tile floors for twenty dollars a month, only to learn that its actual rent is more like ten dollars. What strikes her upon moving in is the "stony bareness" of the house. The kitchen has a cement sink, and there is another in a patio used for laundry, toilet and shower, the whole works packed into a four square foot area.

10/17/74

Dear Mellon,

The name "Oaxaca" has such a mysterious sound, that clattering confusion of the soft start and the sharp ending, the simultaneous signifying of osmosis and penetration. Oaxaca encompasses both a small city where I will live and an outlying valley of seven distinct regions. My friend Harold was right, I will love it here. Oaxaca seems so much more authentically Mexican than anyplace north of Mexico City. The places Eleanor frequents, Puerto Vallarta or Acapulco, are protected tourist colonies for wealthy Americans and adventurous Europeans, mostly French.

A sprawling village of mostly one-story clay houses with garden courtyards. The inhabitants look Mayan and the vibes feel peaceful. The town sits on a plateau, five thousand feet high, surrounded by distant mountains. In the Colonial Spanish center is the *Zócalo*, a huge double square and park with laurel and jacaranda trees and cafés on its borders where people sit for hours with a beer or a coke—no one asks you to leave. At night, there is band music.

Yesterday, I walked all over the town. Streets quickly turn to dirt and you hear braying burros, dogs, and chickens. The Pensione Suiza where I'm staying is located only about eight blocks from the center. I don't need a watch here because the church bells peal on the quarter-hour, an almost omnipresent reminder of "Time's winged chariot" coming near.

The Suiza is owned by the genteel, gnarled, bent Donna

Luiza Martinez. She is over ninety years old but very much in charge, sweet as honey but commanding like a Queen Bee when necessary. She said she did not have a proper room for me so she gave me a long oblong one with sloping ceilings, a small window, and three single beds in file like a military barracks. It faces the Calzada Madero, a noisy street. Oaxaca is not built for the sound of modern transport. The groans and hiccups of trucks echo through the city as if such sounds did not belong. The air is often as full of exhaust fumes as New York City.

The Pensione is ancient and has few amenities: hot water (sometimes only lukewarm) only from eight to ten in the morning. The dining area is clean and the food is plentiful; I hope to get by with breakfast and dinner. The church bells suggest safety. Diet is key: I've already heard many stories of food poisoning, of the various afflictions available to the traveler which become even more dangerous the further south one travels into Central America. Although it is small compensation, the further south one goes, the less expensive everything becomes.

I met Ross Parmenter in the garden before dinner, a lush overgrown area with a small fountain, swaying palm fronds, the fragrance of red frangipani and white honeysuckle, and overhanging bunches of green bananas. Above the garden, forming a square on its edges, is a tiled open terrace crowded with cacti, potted plants, shade, and sun. All the rooms are off the terrace.

Ross looks like he is in his mid-fifties, a ruddy, white haired gentleman who lives here most of the year and who seems to be the resident writer. He was a music editor at the *New York Times* for thirty years, his colleague Gilbert Millstein wrote the rave review that made *On the Road* a bestseller, and he is quite familiar with my subject. He also knew my dissertation adviser, Leon Edel—they are both Canadians. He has written a book about D.H. Lawrence, who lived in Oaxaca and used it as a setting when writing *The Plumed Serpent*. Ross is quite reserved, distant almost, but I hope to learn a lot about Oaxaca from him eventually.

After dinner I met Juan, a young, dark-skinned boy with

chiseled features. Thin, around five foot six, with elegant hands, his demeanor is sensitive, delicate. An exceptionally beautiful descendant of the Mayans, lithe, with gleaming shoulder length ebony hair, Juan looked like a dancer and carried himself with gravity and decorum. He inspired confidence. Kerouac, who was part Mohawk and Iroquois Indian himself, had expressed his admiration in *On the Road* for the indigenous inhabitants of Mexico like Juan "with high cheekbones, slanted eyes, and soft ways".

Juan is here with Nancy, a twenty-eight year old Queens College graduate. Formerly, she administered a welfare office in Keene, New Hampshire. She is three months pregnant and they hope to marry soon. They have had bad things happen to them and she wants to return to the States with him. First, Juan came down with malaria, then they were busted in San Angelo because of her blonde hair. She was jailed for three weeks on a charge of "bad company," then transferred to another jail in Mexico City. Now she has hepatitis. According to Nancy, anyone in Mexico can get arrested on completely fabricated charges that can be dropped with the proper bribes. I loaned her 200 pesos ($15.00) for medicine this morning but she returned the money by afternoon as the check she was expecting arrived.

I don't mean to suggest a grim picture. Oaxaca seems ideal for me. Safety might be more of an issue for you as a woman and with all your photographic equipment. In the *Zócalo*, yesterday, an American told me he only had an Instamatic because a Nikon or Leica was the equivalent of a year's wages in Mexico, and a tempting snatch.

I suspect I haven't given you an accurate view. The street scene is quite lively. Not as many beggars as Mexico City (where the beseeching women asking for alms all seemed very short with small daughters at their sides). Here, women have baskets with produce on their heads; men driving the oldest, most beaten up cars I've seen and so many with detonating mufflers. There are many smiling children but also dour, impassive men who work fourteen hours a day for infinitesimal wages. Oaxaca has been cloudy and the sky a spectacular attraction as the sun keeps trying to emerge. I work on my Spanish in early morning, but forget tomorrow what I learned yesterday so I speak in single word exclamations and point!

Let me know how you are doing, my darling.

Love,
John

10/20/74

Dear Mellon,

I looked at my two pictures of you this morning, and my heart grew warm and sad thinking of you, missing you, wondering what your trip is like—as if I've been away for ages… how are you, darling?

Oaxaca may not be the "sprawling village" I imagined but a small city with strange features, really unlike anything I've seen in Europe. There is much that is very old here, especially the small, squat, soft pastel orange and yellow sun blistered concrete buildings, yet it magically retains a small town atmosphere. I've wandered into the dirt street sections, over crooked cobblestones, nothing over two stories except the churches. Oaxaca has its grand Lady of the Assumption Cathedral and many, many churches with rich altars and carved ceilings.

As Ross Parmenter cheerily suggested to me, however, over breakfast this morning, these are all artifacts of the colonial conquest. The real history is Pre-Columbian, beginning some 15,000 years ago when Asian people, near the end of the last ice age, crossed the Bering Strait, moved south, and settled the Pacific Coast and then pushed east. "Settled," perhaps, is the wrong term for these nomadic hunter-gatherers. Agricultural cultivation of maize, beans, squash, avocados, and chilies began roughly around the time Moses was delivering his Ten Commandments to the Jews in the deserts of the Sinai, more than a thousand years before Christ. The Mayan civilization in Mexico and further south lasted for more than a millennium and achieved a high degree of sophistication in mathematics, astronomy, architecture, and communal organization before Cortez' conquest on horseback and the Spaniards' brutal decision to eliminate any vestiges of what the Zapotecs, the Mixtec, the Aztecs, the Incas in Peru, or other non-Christian and therefore pagan or alien groups had created. The result was cultural destruction, desecration on a major scale, exploitation, and virtual slavery. Ross usually has a smile on his face when he tells me such things, a light touch that seems to lessen the horror.

I'd like to explore as much of this rich history as I can while I'm here, although I can't allow it to distract me from the book I'm trying to write. Ross has loaned me Alexander von Humboldt's *Personal Narrative* for bed-time reading. A friend of Goethe's, Humboldt was an early nineteenth century explorer who charted much of the natural life from Cuba to Venezuela, Peru, and Mexico.

I study my Spanish every morning and I wish I had brought a first-year Spanish primer with me. At meals Juan speaks Spanish to me and I listen to his friends in the *Zócalo*, but it's a bit like swimming in a furious sea, unsuccessfully, grasping for words that resemble English or French. Well, groping in a new language might be good for me while trying to finish and revise my own anxious efforts. One of the reasons I've always wanted to come here was that I heard the culture was different enough to allow me to question my own values, perceptions and preconceptions. The possibility is growth.

Love,
John

10/21/74

Dear Mellon,

Juan is becoming another one of my guides, though he is mysteriously non-verbal, as if he offers some kind of inverse reflection. Of Mayan descent, he does massage and makes flutes. He has an air of grace and the residual innocence of a twenty year old, yet underneath that a latent *brujo* knowledge and, perhaps, power. Juan—John in our language—told me about a brotherhood of friends who lived with him in the mountains, the "cloud-forest," before he met Nancy. He wakes at five to do yoga on the terrace, and is very limber, agile—a native dancer. Yesterday I accompanied him and Nancy to pick up the airline tickets, and then to the vast market that spreads through the streets to find a new shirt that Nancy was buying for him: blue and yellow with little green embroidered pheasants that symbolize freedom because they tend to die in captivity. Juan brought me to a little stand where I could get an authentic *choco haa*, the bitter chocolate of the Mayans, a viscous, concoction made with chili and spices. Was it an initiation?

    Last night, the other young Americans staying at the Pensione Suiza arranged a little departure party. Wine and tequila. Nancy is apprehensive. Her parents in Queens are not receptive to the idea of their Jewish daughter marrying a Mexican, even if, or perhaps because, he descends from an indigenous group. I've been encouraging, but Nancy knows the future may be difficult.

    This afternoon I took them to the airport in a taxi. Juan was so disoriented he forgot his Peruvian sweater jacket, his only warm garment, so we had to return for it. Pallid, weak, and faint, Nancy intends to stay with Quakers in Mexico City until Juan can get his passport, and then fly to New York City. I've spent a lot of time with them in the past few days, trying to help, but now I think I need a little hermitage. I do not know whether I will connect with other friends like Juan and Nancy while I'm here, both of whom crossed my path to assist with cautions and omens. Feel sad though relieved that they have left: real friendship—the ability to respond— involves a lot of responsibility.

The Oaxaca Letters

Just did my laundry in the back yard in two stone tubs with a pail to transport the cold water. One tub is for scrubbing, the other for soaking out the soap. Like the sorcerer's apprentice, lots of trips to get more water. Then, hung my wash in the bright sun on a wire attached to guava trees with limes and banana leaves scattered on the ground. Now I'm at my window looking at the garbage truck—everyone in the area brings their garbage to the garbage haulers so it is a silent process. Ready to get back to work: rereading Burroughs' *Junky* to help determine the influence of Mexico on the Beats twenty-five years ago.

Please give me some news of your spirits. I think of you often, and typing these words my throat tightens and tears seem incipient.

Love,
John

10/24/74

Dear Mellon,

I received the card from Austin, your Medicine Wheel card, and your sweet words made me cry. I will hang it in my new room at the quiet end of the terrace when I move next week and where I can remain until Christmas. I hope you write often, even if just a card, so I can register the details of your days and stay in touch with a reality I can't forget and must always learn to understand.

I do hope you will come down before Christmas. We can take the bus south to San Christobel de las Casas, a charming town in the mountains that Eleanor recommended we visit because of its relatively pure Mayan reminders. It is a difficult journey, twelve hours, a crowded bus that leaves at six am.

I've been working hard despite a head cold since Juan and Nancy's departure, a lot of typing. I finished revising my Ginsberg portrait, went to the *Zócalo* to get it Xeroxed, and sent two separate copies to Joyce Johnson. She may take weeks to reply. I know she is an overworked editor, and my dilemma is that I need to continue with the Kerouac section without her commentary and criticism. She knew both of them intimately and should have a lot to offer.

I took off this afternoon to wander in the market. Bought a small knife to cut fruit, looked at some leather belts, then returned to lie on the terrace in the sun. Will vitamin D dry out the cold? I may be pretty dark when you next see me, but I'll try to get less than an hour a day of direct sun. My cold (caught probably at the goodbye party) has been traveling around the Pensione and is getting steadily worse, phlegm in my throat and last night chills and weakness. My digestion has been fine, and I've had a few coffees in the mornings and an occasional beer. I buy lots of fruit in the *Mercado*—ten times as large as anything we've seen at Bastille in Paris or Arles—for very little money. Today my vitamin C campaign to beat the cold: five oranges, five small apples, and two pounds of bananas all for a total of 75 cents.

Later, I went to the Museo Tamayo, a collection of Pre-Columbian sculpture and pottery, 3000 years old. Tamayo was a Mexican muralist from Oaxaca who collected all these incredible little statues, strangely contorted or grimacing faces with weird noses, twisted upwards sometimes or with a Polynesian stick in them. From one to three feet tall, the bodies can be oddly shaped. The statues are baked, some painted but mostly clay or sand colored. Every room in the museum allows you to hear the relaxing splash of a fountain, and every room has its guard in civilian clothes, usually reading a comic book.

Afterwards, in the *Zócalo*, watching the light change. Slow stroll to Suiza passing blue, pink, green storefronts. Town fairly clean although there are no garbage cans. Early tomorrow morning, the streets will be swept with brooms. I will hear the straw brushing at dawn like a sort of gentle breathing.

The Oaxaca Letters

But by now it is 6:30p.m., quite dark and time for supper at Suiza: chicken à la king and overcooked peas with carrots, roll, apple sauce, sweet roll for desert, and manzanilla tea. There are few guests in the dining room. At one table, Donna Luisa's husband in a wheelchair is assisted by his aide. At another is Ross Parmenter, who asks how my day has gone, but his query seems formal, almost delivered as courtesy. He works most of the day on the terrace outside his room, his typewriter clattering like a woodpecker on amphetamines. He is writing a biography of Zenia Nuttall, a nineteenth century anthropologist. While he eats, he reads, with furrowed brow. At her own table is Joan Kantor, another permanent resident, a dumpy but very sweet artist from Philadelphia with a little dog named Ruby. Finally, at yet another table sits Virginia, an elderly artist from Ventura, California. She was raised in Shanghai before the revolution where her father was a biology professor.

The room is so quiet one can hear us all chewing and swallowing. The conversation is quite spare: it could set a scene for a Beckett play about the sound of silence.

There are six other young Americans in the Pensione who are not present; perhaps $2 for dinner is too much compared to what one can get in the market? Missing are a couple from Colorado, another from upper New York, and two raw, brassy Alaskan ladies, Peggy and her companion, a plump, boisterous woman who announces herself as Kodiak Rose.

Love,
John

Beat Transnationalism

10/27/74

Dear Mellon,

How are you my love? I think of you so often. This morning I showed your picture to the two Alaskan women, and told them about your adventurous spirit. There seems to be something mismatched about these two young women. Peggy is a lanky blonde with a leer; essentially a sweet but dumb farm girl looking for a good time. Rose is short, fiery, and quick. She was married and told me she wants to sterilize herself. Doesn't it seem strange that she would want to share such a matter with me?

    I decided to take off to visit Monte Alban, the former seat of Zapotec power in the region. A half an hour bus ride, climbing all the way, hairpin turns like Equinox in Vermont, until we reach a large flat mesa with pyramid structures. Ross told me archeological evidence determines the mountaintop was leveled around 600B.C.—a considerable engineering feat—and irrigation, sanitation, and food provided for a population estimated at over 40,000 inhabitants. A center of Mesoamerican civilization, it had once bustled with master builders, traders, and vendors, warriors and slaves, and the astronomer-priests who organized Zapotec daily life with their sacred and secular calendars. The city provided a market for jaguar skins, quetzal feathers, obsidian, and seashells. Its influence radiated for two hundred miles in any direction of the Oaxaca valley, but the city was suddenly and mysteriously abandoned in the ninth century A.D., long before the Spanish arrived.

    I saw large stones—how had they been dragged so high?—with rough engravings, though nothing like the carving I saw in the Museo Tamayo. I was particularly impressed by one frieze of a Zapotec woman in a seated position giving birth. The pyramids have openings, small tunnels that quickly turn pitch black, a darkness so absolute and frightening. I found one tunnel that emerged—after several feet of groping through the narrow dirt passage—in a stone room with a high apex shaped like a triangle where I sat on a stone floor in silent awe. It reminded me of the human transience Ginsberg describes when he spent a night alone in the ruins at Chichén Itzá and saw thousand year old stone phalli covered with moss and bat shit.

    I wandered about the monumental ruins in the hot sun for a few hours. There were remnants of temples, palaces, marketplaces, large funerary urns, an oblong ball court. This was where the Zapotecs played a curiously non-competitive game, more like a dance than Lacrosse, with huge balls larger than a basketball, made from the sap of the *Castilloa* tree, which the players would jostle with hips and rear-ends up and down the court. Later, in the more competitive Aztec version, some losers could be ritually sacrificed.

                                         Love,
                                         John

                                         10/28/74

Dear Mellon,

Sunday, after yoga, instead of breakfast, I took off for the market, the huge street procession that goes on for blocks and blocks through the center of town. Started my day with a *jugo*, a fresh drink for 25 cents made in a blender of any fruits you desire: papaya, mango, banana, or orange. It is safe because no water or ice is added so no abdominal distress—*tourista*.

    You could spend days photographing here: carts loaded with herbs, nuts, and spices, fruits and vegetables, flowers, hung meats and fowl, leather goods, necklaces, sandals and hats, household supplies, hammocks, pottery. Everywhere you look you see chunks of limestone used for grinding corn, giant piles of maize, peppers, beans, squashes, onions, tomatoes, avocados and potatoes, a dozen different types of chilies, papayas, guavas, red cactus fruits, sacks of cocoa and coffee beans. Imagine a city block of garlic, hundreds of women sitting in the street with their wares, men pushing themselves through crowded aisles with handcarts, all in a gloriously psychedelic profusion of color—the orange, yellow, red, and scarlet and bright green of the produce. The scope, volume, and variety of this *mercado* is overwhelming. How does one return to a mall/supermarket culture after this?

How different the Oaxaca market seems when compared to the night walks through blocks of street vendors whose stands are illuminated by candles, dim bulbs, and lanterns Kerouac describes in *Tristessa*. The rhythm of his sentences soar and his view is exultant but phantasmagoric. He was also living on pennies a day, very close to a vagrant's perspective, and dangerously in love with a prostitute-addict who was subject to the sexual whims of the Chief of Police in Mexico City. Such an association might help to explain the sinister edge of Kerouac's descriptions.

Later, in the *Zócalo,* met an American couple that had just returned from Panajachel in Guatemala where my friend Harold Jaffe is—Hal who recommended Oaxaca to me as a place in which I could work. They said a volcano had recently erupted and the ash was all over, in the air, in one's hair, making breathing difficult.

Still, I'm thinking it might be a destination for us when you come down. Then met a blond American named Marcus carrying a dulcimer in a patchwork leather sack. He invited me to his home, an hour bus ride away, but told me there would be no returning bus until the following day. When I refused, he flashed a card that fit in his palm that proclaimed, "I want to suck your cock!" I told him his method was quaint, but my preference for the present was celibacy, that Buddhists believe that storing semen leads to creative expression.

Love,
John

The Oaxaca Letters

10/29/74

Dear Mellon,

Chatted with Miriam Joel, a German Jew staying briefly in the Pensione. She knew Henry Miller in Paris in the thirties, met Nin but disliked her intensely, felt she was so pretentious, an actress and insincere, the opposite of Miller. She escaped the Nazis, lived in New York, knew Paul Goodman and Fritz Perls, but has spent the last forty years in Lima, Peru. She claims it is a particularly repressive place, and the government will only allow one to leave with enough money for a four-week holiday. She spoke so quickly and so much I could hardly manage a word.

Last night went to the *Zócalo* with Kodiak Rose and Peggy, the two flashy Alaskan women in the Pensione. Their raucous eagerness to invite any adventure makes me cautious around them. They worked in the fishing industry in plants where fish is processed. No women on the boats where the real money can be earned, but they saved enough to come here. Yet, like many of the footloose Americans I've met in Mexico, they are improvident and spend recklessly. They are down to their last $50 and waiting for money from home. I loaned them $5.00 until their money arrives. They seem to take great comfort in the loan, as if they had earned it.

What one may quickly realize when abroad is how comfortable life can be in the States. I know you realize this because of your letters last year from Surinam. Well, you traveled three hundred miles down the Saramacca River in a dugout canoe so you have a better idea of discomfort than I do. Even our summer haven in Vermont, our old collapsing farmhouse on the hill, with its wildflowers and outhouse, offers more comfort to me than any place south of the Rio Grande. Are you planning to visit Vermont? Remember to write and share the most intimate or petty details. Nothing you can tell me will seem uninteresting. I think of you with love and know you will always be the most important part of my life.

                                                  Love,
                                                  John

                                                  10/31/74

Dear Mellon,

Recurrent dreams of driving for hours in a car, totally misdirected, on the wrong road, arriving too late for departing trains, of finding myself at the wrong destination, knocking on the wrong door, anxious, lost.

    Are such night sweat dreams related to my speculations, to the book I'm trying to write? Last year, interviewing the poet Allen Ginsberg in his apartment on East 12th Street in Manhattan, I told him about my unease with what I consider the two Ur-origins of the Beat story. First, David Kammerer is murdered by Lucien Carr in Riverside Park near Columbia University in 1944, causing Kerouac and Burroughs to collaborate on a fiction about that event, and Ginsberg to write his *Journal of the Fall* that I was allowed to read in the Columbia University Ginsberg archive. Second, William Burroughs shoots his common-law wife, and the mother of his son, at close range in Mexico City in 1951.

    I asked Ginsberg, with particular reference to Burroughs, how to identify, or convince, a general public to sympathize, or at least understand such an act?

    His reply was baffling: "You won't understand us unless you've lived in Mexico" which is why I am here.

    Yes, I do find Burroughs' fiction terrifying, more so than

The Oaxaca Letters

Conrad or Kafka. Carnival humor doesn't provide relief from the terror of human reversion to an amoeboid state. The sense of death in his work is so omnipresent, the flatness of nightmares and scenes of incredible violence like the kids burning a bum early in *Naked Lunch*. The terror is not suspenseful as in Poe's "Masque of the Red Death" but almost pornographic, bodies ripped asunder, decapitation or castration as frequent as breakfast toast. Right now I'm trying to understand the remarkable shift that occurs in Burroughs' evolution as a novelist from the cool anthropological perspective of his first novel, *Junky*, a traditional narrative written during the year of his trial in Mexico City, to the heated post-modernist swirl of his masterpiece, *Naked Lunch*. Is the drastic change a consequence of drug use combined with the emotional devastation caused by the shooting?

And I have so many doubts that the event, a version of the Willem Tell fable, was accidental. They were at a party, their relationship was tortured, there was alcohol and probably drugs, she was eight feet away, and Burroughs was a crack shot. His family hired the slickest lawyer in Mexico City, who probably coached the witnesses. Ginsberg told me he thinks Joan had been damaged by amphetamines and was playing a version of suicide by cop. It almost seems like a rationalization.

Happy Halloween,
John

11/1/74

Dear Mellon,

Received your news that Aunt Lillian is remarrying. First news for me. Was there another letter (which may not have reached me)? All I have is the Medicine Wheel card and this letter.

Interesting that you have the possibility of an assignment doing photographs of the Oaxaca Valley. You will be carrying what might represent a fortune in camera equipment to the poor farming people who live in the valley. A car can be rented for around thirty dollars a day, but you would need a driver. Ross told me the Zapotecs and Miztecs had built irrigation systems. He said there was a small dam between Huayapan and Tlalixtac, and another called Jalapo del Marques. The big dam in the area is in the northeast, Cerro de Auro (hill of gold) located above Tuxepec. Too bad we don't know how to use a gun because it might be dangerous for us in the mountains. I've heard in the gossip at the *Zócalo* that there is still human sacrifice in the region. So if the *federales* don't shake you down, the locals may have you for lunch. I realize this may seem exaggerated to you but I am reading *Naked Lunch*, which incorporates versions of the ritual sacrifice and torture Burroughs studied while at Mexico City College in 1950.

I'll just share one story I heard since today is the Day of the Dead. Last night, we had a small Halloween birthday party for Kodiak Rose. I bought a dozen roses and a shawl, all for less than a dollar. Rose and Peggy's room is still decorated with the crepe decorations I draped for Juan and Nancy's departure. We all drank mescal and ate chocolate cake.

At the party, I met a man named Michael, from Second Avenue and Sixth St., a few blocks from where we lived in Manhattan when we met. He shared a mesmerizing rap. He is from North Dakota, where his mother worked as an Indian agent and where he learned how to ride and train horses. He never graduated high school and has been on the road for eight years, a member of Kerouac's "rucksack revolution." He spent a year in India searching for miracles. Once he met a *sadhu*, a holy wanderer (although to western eyes a beggar) who was pestering him for alms. When Michael was reluctant to give anything, the *sadhu* said he would show him something for some money. He had long, dry, matted white hair that he squeezed hard, producing water. Was it a trick or a miracle?

Michael was here to get supplies, but he expressed great

hatred for Oaxaca City. He has been apprehended on several occasions by omnipresent federal police, the *federales* who need income to supplement their meager salaries. He suggests the ransom number is the biggest game in Mexico, and, even in Mexico City, the Mayor's son has been kidnapped and held until the police got their raises. Five years ago, most people did not lock their doors and cars were left unlocked. On a recent visit, he said, his car windows were smashed and the stereo removed. Once, he was mugged on the streets even though he knows karate and carries a knife.

Now he lives on an isolated ranch in the mountains two hours away, which he purchased for $6000. He drives there, but can only reach his place with another arduous climb on foot or horseback. He makes money by breaking wild horses and illustrating children's books sent to him by an agent in San Francisco. It does seem like an unlikely combination.

He has lived with some of the local descendants of the Maya, and learned to speak their indigenous languages. He was introduced to psychedelic mushrooms by some of his new mountain friends, although he admits few Indians eat mushrooms. Tribal medicine men, called witch doctors by the priests, *brujos* or *curanderos* (healers) in Spanish, often use mushrooms although few have genuine powers. He claims to have met some who do, though. Once, when he was not high himself, the *curandero* predicted an animal would enter the room and then a weasel walked in which he fondled. Another time, hundreds of toads manifested, hopping about the room. He said another regional practice of the *brujos* is to catch vampire bats, break their wings, and allow them to heal in a box. Then the *brujo* commands the bat to fly, usually to deliver sickness to a particular person.

Michael eats mushrooms in tombs. He was taught by companions to fast prior to ingestion; sometimes they fast for a week before. Then he told me a frightening story of how his seventeen-year-old Indian wife found a tomb with pottery that she took. A few days later her body swelled up and she died and her brother, who had committed the theft with her, had an eye shot out in a dispute a week later. Michael ate mushrooms and went back to the tomb to return the pottery.

So it was a fascinating birthday party and I remained until 2a.m.

Love,
John

11/2/74

Dear Mellon,

Dry, clear, blazing sun above. My stomach seems in balance, no more acidity due to insecurity, the fear of articulating something meaningful and writing it well.

I've moved to room nine, in the far corner of the terrace, a spacious room with a double bed, good light, my own bathroom, and much less noise than I had to endure when I was facing the avenue.

If Joyce ever sends me her comments, it will be a delightful workroom. This week I moped my way through my manuscript once again. Also read *Ancient Oaxaca*,[1] a lot of which was technical archeology, and I guess I'm uninterested in the speculative dating of tombs and pottery. There is a genocidal history here though: it is estimated that a population of twenty million people was reduced to less than a million after Cortez, the decimation in part due to disease brought by the Spaniards, so a kind of unintentional germ warfare? The Zapotecs were called

---

1   Paddock, John, and Bernal, Ignacio, *Ancient Oaxaca,* Stanford University Press, 1966

"cloud people" because some of them lived at high elevations. The name Oaxaca, with its curious clashing ring, derives from a bean-like fruit from a tree. The indigenous name for the fruit is "huaxyucac," in Spanish called *guaje*; outside of towns, many people only speak the old languages.

Last night I couldn't sleep so read Humboldt's *Personal Narrative* which helped me to see how the indigenous peoples of South America were more advanced than the Spanish colonialists could ever admit. The myth behind western imperialism is what Kipling acknowledged as the "white man's burden": give the barbarians Jesus as salve for slavery. Humboldt is a scientific observer who seems usually reluctant to consider the personal dimensions of his travels by sea and on land. But what he records are the habits of Indians living among crocodiles, mosquitoes, and monkeys as in this fascinating gem I discovered at the end of chapter fourteen:

> The Indians often find enormous boas, which they call *uji*, or water snakes, in a similar state of lethargy. To revive them they sprinkle the boas with water. They kill them and hang them in a stream, and after they have rotted they make guitar strings from the tendons on their dorsal muscles, which are far better than strings made from howler-monkey guts.

This morning set out with Virginia, the elderly artist who lives here, for Tlacalula, but we got to the bus station too late to board the bus. Last night Virginia took a young Canadian named Daniel and me to a dance at the medical school, a very crowded bus ride to the outskirts of town, standing all the way. She felt claustrophobic so we walked the last half-mile. Adjacent to the medical school was an illuminated multi-colored fountain with sculptures of seven women, each one dressed in another regional outfit. One was topless, which Virginia said was customary in that section.

Everything is late in Mexico and there was a crowd

inside, entire families, even babies, probably mostly middle class because the school is located in a good residential neighborhood. The dance was a Day of the Dead ceremony, performed by students from the university's art school. It began very slowly with a brass band and a candlelight procession to a nearby cemetery. The setting was framed by tall cypress trees and, between gravestones, a tall altar was supported by sugar cane stalks and heaped with fruit, candles, and incense. Figures in white robes appeared with grinning death masks—the risen dead—and began their dance, first slowly, then picking up speed and whirling about. Some had skeletons stenciled on their tights, others wore skirts, all trying to rouse the spectators who seemed rooted in silent prayer. The strobe lights made the ghosts flicker with magical momentum. Several red devils with pitchforks tried to drag spectators and children off, and another skeletal figure with a large scythe kept weaving through the dancers. The event, with its combination of elegance and eerie frenzy, with the evident belief of the community in the veneration of the dead, evoked old ways of animist origins.

Love, John

The Oaxaca Letters

11/3/74

Dear Mellon,

Had breakfast with Daniel, who has some astonishing stories. Tense, questioning, but full of pessimistic gloom, a high school dropout from Vancouver, he spent the last two years in Bermuda playing bass in a rock band where he met two Dutch brothers and an ailing Englishman and his wife who invited him to sail to the Azores. It is a long haul but, incredibly, no one on board had *any* experience sailing. They spent more than a month in a forty-five foot boat with an inoperable radio tossed about in perpetually stormy seas. Someone had to manage the rudder at all times, and they needed to catch fish for food for the last two weeks. Daniel lost twenty-five pounds. He still seems to be tossed about, uncertain of what to do with his future. He writes tiny plaintive songs that he sings to me.

Later, I read on the terrace, mostly light stuff like an article in *Commentary* by William Barrett on his friendship with the poet Delmore Schwartz. I stayed out of the sun since my skin is still peeling because of my hatless visit to Monte Alban.

I did reread my portrait of Kerouac though and still wonder what Joyce disliked about it. She is rarely precise or detailed, which makes me wonder how carefully she reads my material. Perhaps she has insufficient time? I think she disdains conventional criticism but the *Partisan Review* and *American Scholar* pieces I used to get my contract are much more than that.

I did send her a telegram asking her to respond, at least, to the Ginsberg section I sent previously. I think she could let things slide, hoping I reach some epiphany about my material before then. I did complete a twelve hundred-word introduction to the biographical sections that frame the material effectively. At least, I think so, but I do need confirmation.

In the late afternoon went to the *Zócalo* to enjoy a solitary beer. Everyone in their finery, men in turquoise trousers, balloons flying, the city quiet without its buses belching black smoke. In the center, in the gazebo with its dome, cupola, and metal fretwork, a marimba band played xylophones. I feel my freakiness more than ever here because of Mexican stares of amazement. It isn't my long hair, I suspect, but the beard, which is equated with revolution and perhaps because men here can't often develop beards until after fifty. So I'm one hundred now! I don't feel fear although a Mexican policeman gave me the wrong directions to a museum the other day, and occasionally I hear the epithet of "loco" shouted from a passing car.

                Love,
                John

11/4/74

Dear Mellon,

Went to Mitla with Virginia, who knows the area well. She reminds me of a chicken so I laughed to myself when a package containing dead chicken began to drip through the roof of the old bus. On the way—a twenty-five mile trip—the bus stopped for ten minutes at El Tule, a huge bald cypress, tall as a ten-story building, with a tremendous girth, almost two hundred feet at its base. When the scientist Alexander von Humboldt visited it in 1803, he estimated that it was four thousand years old. It must have been a ceremonial center for the Mesoamericans who settled this area. We exited briefly at the stop where women were selling water we could not drink.

    Dry corn in the fields grown in semi-arid land being harvested by machete. No machines in sight; farmers guiding plows pulled by oxen in the hot fields. Mitla is a large town with dirt streets. The church has three bleeding Christs, one dark skinned, another lying in a sort of bier with blood on his forehead and lips. The town, like much of old Mexico, is built of adobe, a fusion of clay, round stones, corn stalks, and animal dung. Some houses have thatched roofs, with succulent pink flowering plants; some are bordered by hedges of organ-pipe cactus, a serried, upright barrier. There were boys walking burros, forlorn women gazing out of tiny windows without glass, roosters promenading freely, what looked like stray mongrels everywhere, women in the market selling marigolds and cockscombs, big and red like carnations. Now, the rainy season is over and flowers peak. People here seem much friendlier than in Oaxaca, which Virginia says has been spoiled by tourism.

She brought me to see the Pre-Columbian collection of a friend, Howard Leigh. He is a doddering old American who has been here since 1945 and has an amazing group of statues, three-foot high facemasks worn by priests. Some objects are three thousand years old. A profusion of vases and bowls, figurines and headdresses, one anguished woman with holes for eyes. Leigh has loaned some of these objects to the Metropolitan Museum of Art, hoping they might be broken, he confided, so he could collect the insurance. He cannot sell his objects and they cannot leave Mexico otherwise.

The ruins are a half a mile walk out of town. The conquistadores often razed entire cities, and built their central churches using the stones of the temple complexes that preceded their conquest. Here, remnants of the ruins have survived though the spectacle is much less imposing than Monte Alban. There is one palatial ruin still standing with very low doorways and intricately designed hexagonal and pentagonal patterns decorating the ceilings. I saw no friezes or exterior stone carvings, though I was startled when I entered one humid cave to see a Mexican man vigorously dry humping another.

Love,
John

11/5/74

Dear Mellon,

Just received your letter postmarked 10/21. I think one or two of your letters may have gone awry in the Mexican mail. I wrote to Hal in Guatemala for news of the volcano but no answer, perhaps due to the unreliability of mail service. I've been writing to you almost daily, keeping carbons as an epistolary diary, what you did in Surinam when you were living with the Chinese family.

    Last night, asleep by 10P.M., there was a knock on my door. Juan reappeared. He told me he had left Nancy in Mexico City and had a letter from her to deliver. She is still in Mexico City with the Quaker House of Amigos and they have given her a job as a typist. His story seems peculiar: he got his passport, but the American Embassy refused him an entry visa because he has neither job nor savings. He plans to meet up with Nancy, somehow, in San Diego—all I can suppose is an illicit border crossing. He is in Oaxaca, he claims, because he has to get penicillin for a sick friend with syphilis living in the mountains near San José del Pacifico (a known dope center), four hours from here. He has been in Mexico City for only a few weeks but he seems changed, unhealthy somehow, his eyes narrowed, his face puffed, a worried look. He slept in my room and departed early, getting the medicine and returning to San Jose.

    Today I reread my Kerouac section again—still no word from Joyce so I'm somewhat in the dark. Unsure about how to satisfy her. She knew Kerouac so intimately, was a girlfriend during the period that *On the Road* was published, and has let me read their subsequent correspondence.

    This afternoon, I watched a large banana tree get cut down in the courtyard because it had a ripe bunch. Two years for a tree to produce, huge six-foot leaves, and only one bunch per tree. Taste is fruity and a bit mushy. Then, Rose and Peggy showed up. Donna Luisa had asked them to leave the Pensione because they were inviting men to their room. They, coincidentally I wonder, had just come back from San José del Pacifico where they had been mercilessly harassed by young Mexican boys who

The Oaxaca Letters

had invited them to stay. Rose said they loved it near the top of a mountain, at an altitude over ten thousand feet and freezing most nights. We all had a smoke, Peggy showered, said it was now her birthday, and they left.

Then Daniel reappeared with his friend Joseph and they jammed on one guitar and sang some blues by candlelight. A few minutes later, Rose and Peggy came back. Rose has been around, traveled a lot in Spain and Morocco where her former husband, Paul, babysat a hash farm. She claims Moroccans hate white Christians, will spit at you if given the opportunity. Women are systematically mistreated: old women transporting huge bundles on foot while their sons supervise sitting on donkeys.

They seem to regard me as a reliable friend, perhaps because I've loaned them some small amounts of money that they haven't yet repaid. The bank claims their money still hasn't arrived and they asked for another $20. It is a familiar story told by Americans in Mexico: even Virginia explained she had to wait six weeks for a check to clear she knew had arrived.

Perhaps Rose and Peggy consider me as an ally because I must be the only guy in Oaxaca who hasn't come on to them sexually? I have remained celibate—and I would never get near them because syphilis is so rampant here. Rose and Peggy are very loose ladies, but tough and spirited.

After an hour or so of talking, Peggy saw that a three-inch jet-black scorpion had somehow crawled into my room. I've seen green geckoes immobile on the walls but this apparition was frightening, a sign right out of William Burroughs' universe where the scorpions take over Times Square. In a fluent Zen parry, Rose just scooped the scorpion up with a page from my manuscript and put it outside my door, saying it should not be killed. Maybe it was a traffic cop?

Love,
John

11/6/74

Dear Mellon,

How are you, *primero amigo des dias en munde,* whom I love only?

Some of the Mayan female faces are wide open with an expression like subdued longing. Henrietta, who does the rooms and serves the meals, and everyone else here, has such a mooning face. She, Ross, and Virginia always ask how my work is going. When Henrietta doesn't hear me typing, she wonders whether I "enscribo hoy?" Ross Parmenter is always posing esthetic questions, quaintly pursing his lips as he tries to fashion his words fastidiously.

Of course, I can't know how my work goes until I hear from Joyce, and I haven't. Otherwise, I might set off one of those "fabulous roman candles exploding like spiders in the stars" which Kerouac imagines near the beginning of *On the Road* to characterize his eager generation. My roman candle right now is sputtering.

I strangely keep remembering our little hilltop farmhouse in Vermont, the Taurean part of me that delights in the neighboring heifers, the openness of our undisturbed retreat there, the simple pleasures of walking up and down the dirt road and finding a new wildflower every day in June, or discovering the pig and its litter of half a dozen little piglets at Burr's farm?

I can't imagine anything here as idyllic as what we have in Vermont. Perhaps it is due to linguistic inadequacy—my Spanish still on the level of very basic communication—but down deep I suspect many Mexican people are not fond of Americans. We seized half their country once and now visit as tourists who, as Burroughs advises, are often seen as prey here. Mexican men tend to be macho and domineering, and women are disregarded or subjected. There really is such a thing as a cultural division that one does not feel in Europe, although we saw how awfully the Muslim women were treated in the southern part of Yugoslavia.

As Burroughs wrote in a letter to Kerouac in the early 1950s,

The Oaxaca Letters

Mexico was "still an Oriental country that reflects two thousand years of disease and poverty and degradation and stupidity and slavery and brutality and psychic and physical terrorism." He goes on to say that Mexico is sinister and gloomy with the special chaos of dreams; of course, he was addicted, writing *Junky*, and although I can see his perspective is more partial and subjective than representative, I have to respect its applicability, its partial or potential truth.

Anyway, I'm just riding the air now, staying close to the Pensione, reading and writing. Ross loaned me his copy of Malcolm Lowry's *Under the Volcano* which is situated in this region. Lowry's language is fascinating, as liberated, intoxicated really, as Joyce's or Kerouac's. I want to get my own impressions of Mexico down on paper too, no matter whether anyone wants to print what I transcribe. The activity is the natural extension of my mind; the way to actively engage it. That, after all, is the instrument I have chosen to play; the music I need to make in this lifetime.

Love,
John

11/7/74

Dear Mellon,

So glad you liked the *Partisan Review* interview I did with Ginsberg. I'm also so glad I decided not to use my original, overblown introduction. Be more reticent, you advised. Remember, it was just serendipity that it occurred at all when we were in Cherry Valley visiting him? He had me picking beans the first day, and in the evening I gave him a draft of the critical section on Burroughs. The next morning he wanted to discuss it and you had the presence of mind to suggest I use the tape recorder. The interview offers, I think, the best critical understanding we have so far of Burroughs' peculiar cosmogony, much more clarifying than Eric Mottram's clotted commentary.[2] It is quite different from the ones I did with John Holmes, Carl Solomon or Huncke.

    All the angry resentment I directed at you last spring seems to have dissipated, and I, too, only want to restore the bonds. I hope if we learn to compromise, we can build our own uniquely free relationship together, work together, help each other. We may have different ambitions, but we share a profound mutual love that should be enough to surmount any obstacles, some of which we ourselves in our self-destructive passions have created.

    I think when I began this book I just got drunk with my own potential and power. I think the distance Mexico has afforded—not even a telephone connection to you or anyone else—has allowed me to measure the shallowness of my own pretentions. Funny how being so far away allows one to discover a crucial inner perspective, to distinguish qualities simply smothered by routine and familiar surroundings. Part of what I'm feeling—the diminishment of ego and ambition—may be due to the vacuum caused by Joyce's silence. I sent her yet another desperate plea yesterday, another message in a bottle sucked into a void? I move through my days without regret or sadness, but free of the debilitating hilarity of New York.

---

2   PARTISAN REVIEW, vol. xli, no2 pp.253-62

The Oaxaca Letters

Yesterday, I slowly retyped and rewrote the introduction to my biographical portrait of Kerouac, but I don't see how to improve the critical section. Frustrated, at around three in the afternoon, I walked to San Domingo, the grand church built by the Spanish in the center of town with some of the gold they had seized. The Zapotecs only used gold as a decorative object, not as a source of financial value. The vaulted ceiling is maybe a hundred feet high. Every inch that isn't devoted to painting or sculpture is covered by gold leaf or filigree. It seems like a huge glittering cavern that progresses beyond mere gaudiness to camp.

Walking back to the *Zócalo*, I saw Juan sitting with Peggy. He looked faded and unwell. They were sitting with an emaciated man with a shaved head from Wisconsin, called Lehigh. He was extremely pallid and in the fading light his skin had an almost phosphorescent hue. There was a bottle of wormy mescal on the table and a few glasses. Lehigh poured me a shot. Then he gave Peggy a thin stack of peso notes and she left to accompany Juan to the bus station as he was returning to San José del Pacifico. I remained to hear Lehigh's bizarre rap.

He spoke so rapidly, leaving so many words out, I thought he was on amphetamines. He said he traveled throughout South America to buy embroideries, and old woven bags and baskets that he shipped back to Milwaukee. Said he made a good living, but Mexico was ruled by "mordida" and he had to bribe everyone in the process, from baggage clerks to the customs police. He said, and Burroughs confirms this in *Junky,* that many Mexicans, especially the more affluent, walked around with a loaded pistol. If stopped by police, the worst that would happen is that the policeman would confiscate your weapon, and perhaps even try to resell it to you.

Previously, he had chosen to follow Burroughs' path to Columbia, Ecuador, and Peru in search of *ayahuasca*, a psychedelic vine potentially inducing telepathic states administered by *curanderos*. Lehigh met many Americans on the same trail; many were simply nuts, some of them were genuinely seeking enlightenment after reading a book called

The Secret of the Andes. He met a former student of the botanist, Professor Schultes at Harvard, who had dropped out. Some wandered the Andes for quasi-religious reasons. One of them may have been another friend Lehigh described, a chemist who believed that the gravity field around the Equator would make it possible—with heavy doses of yagé and another drug, DMT—to enter the fourth dimension. He tried hard, but only succeeded in damaging his nervous system.

Lehigh said he spent months unsuccessfully searching for a mysterious city in the jungle when he met someone he called "Crazy Richard" who was fleeing a drug indictment for manufacturing a million doses of LSD. In Colombia in 1968, with a few like-minded friends, Richard began giving the acid away and some poor Colombians climbed telephone poles screaming for Mama. The attitude of Colombians changed from welcome the hippy with peace to hostility and guns.

I had the feeling that Lehigh's stories could go on forever, or at least as long as the mescal lasted. He sounded a bit like one of the deranged characters in Burroughs' fiction, zigzagging from one tall tale to another. Walking back to the Pensione, I wondered whether it was incorrect to introduce myself as a writer. So many of the travelers I met had such wild tales of misadventure in Mexico and further south. For them, did I represent a sort of confessional priest capable of absolution? Many had certainly asked for advice. Was I a repository for their histories, a well into which they could secret their jewels in a time of peril?

Love,
John

The Oaxaca Letters

11/8/74

Dear Mellon, my love,

Worked desultorily, going over my material so often I almost have memorized it. Rose came over to invite me to dinner and repay the loans—was it Lehigh's money transfer yesterday? I spent the rest of the afternoon writing to Hal who is leaving Guatemala because the volcano rerouted traffic in front of his house. So he is going to Columbia and points south.

At dinner, Rose brought another traveler whom she was treating, and like all the others I seemed to meet he had a harrowing tale that he shared with what seemed a compulsive ardor between gulps of beans and rice. He had been sitting on the benches that fringe the *Zócalo* with two friends at around eleven the night before. Suddenly, a *federale* in street clothes came up from behind as another tossed a bag of grass from a cruising civilian car into his lap. The *federales* wanted a thousand pesos for each American, but the boys talked them into accepting just one thousand pesos for all—that was all the money they had left.

I was beginning to feel a bit like Coleridge's Ancient Mariner burdened by tales of woe when another man stopped at our table to ask whether I taught at Queens College. Dominick Yezzo was a former student. He had been to Vietnam and had a war diary published about his experiences there. He had been in Mexico for two months, had been shaken down by police once, and bitten by scorpions on an island in the Pacific Coast, so he got quite ill. Then, with a girlfriend on the beach at Puerto Escondido, they were accosted by several men who claimed to be police, two of whom tried to rape his friend.

Dominick said he was convinced that Mexicans hate *gringos,* and this remark was overheard by a Mexican at the next table who joined us with another bottle. This often can become a tricky scene, especially when one is invited to drink and does not have the inclination or the fortitude. Jaime Capilla, however, was not insistent, but a government pilot, and he proudly showed us his identification card. Middle class Mexicans, he admitted, disparage the *Indios,* and dislike young footloose Americans. American women are regarded as whores because so many of them come to Mexico with promiscuous intentions. Unlike most Mexicans, he did not despise indigenous people. He lived for a period in a Huicholes village, a tribe never subdued by either the *conquistadores* or the Mexican government. During the first year that he lived in the village no one would even speak to him, but by his third year he was eating mushrooms with them. We talked until midnight while he kept drinking.

Rose and Peggy are leaving for Guatemala soon. Their departure makes me aware of the virtual nature of my experience here thus far. To resort to academic jargon, it has been more dependent on secondary sources than the primacy of actual discovery—the hitchhiking in *On the Road,* for example, traversing the U.S. in all its beautiful variety, Sal picking cotton with Terry, going to jazz bars with Dean, even the soiled sojourn at the end of the novel in a Mexican whorehouse.

When you arrive in Oaxaca, carnival should be beginning and this place will seem less tranquil. I've heard all these distressing cautionary stories, and Jaime Capilla confirmed the rumor I heard that there could very well be a post-Christmas sweep of Americans by the *federales.*

It all makes me want to leave Oaxaca as soon as your assignment on the irrigation system is completed. I care much less about Joyce's deferred comments and completion of my book will just have to wait until she is ready. She is editing six books now. Maybe books take off like airplanes waiting for permission to leave at an airport: maybe the fog in McGraw-Hill's schedule means my book will appear later than I expected.

Hal's move to Columbia and Rose and Peggy's imminent move to Guatemala inspire me. The travelers I meet here are transient and like those in *On the Road,* they are MOVING!

I miss our profound communion and hope we can move together soon.

                                              Love,
                                              John

The Oaxaca Letters

11/9/74

Dear Mellon,

I feel relaxed, a placid glow inside, a soothing presence. I am quite aware as well of an ominous edge of danger that may lurk outside the comforts of the Pensione—the shadowy apprehension of implacable evil just over his shoulder that Burroughs evokes so often in his fiction, or that it is so pervasive in *Under the Volcano*.

Lowry's novel is a must read, by the way, an amazing but neglected masterpiece like Paul Bowles' *The Sheltering Sky*. Lowry's main character, Geoffrey Firmin, is an infirm alcoholic suffering from a year's separation from his younger wife, Yvonne, a former actress, and his own rapid dissolution. He had resigned from the British diplomatic service in 1938, a year or so before the action of the novel begins, when Mexico nationalized its oil and Britain broke relations.

In the beginning of the novel, Yvonne is expected to return, but so is Firmin's younger brother Hugh, whose previous affair with Yvonne helped dissolve their bonds. Each chapter is told through another consciousness (like Robert Browning's *The Ring and the Book*) but the dominating force is Firmin's deterioration, his periods of *delirium tremens,* the terror of his hallucinations and the sheer pathos of his imaginary conversations. The novel's unbelievable intensity is due to Firmin's voice, his wildly obsessive subjectivity, his awful emotional blindness, the result of an extended "horripilating hangover" to use Lowry's innovative language, and because most of its action occurs on the Day of the Dead. Words, entire phrases, are repeated creating a tolling, fatalistic rhythm. His drinking seems even more intense than Kerouac's and Lowry died of it a decade after writing the book just as Kerouac did twelve years after the publication of *On the Road*.

Yesterday, I returned to the *Zócalo* for a farewell dinner with Peggy and Rose. The tacos were too hot, the cheese too salty, the chicken enchiladas passable; the food in Mexico seems mediocre and frequently over spiced, perhaps as a disguise? Rose, apparently, had invited Jaime Capilla, the airline pilot who joined us a half an hour later, and invited all of us to a party.

It may not have been quite what we expected. There were three other airline pilots and an older man who said he was an aerial photographer in a hotel suite, all drinking rum and cokes. They seemed quite stoned and one of them admitted he had to leave in an hour on a late flight. Everything seemed copacetic for the first hour as Jaime, who had been part of a Mexican rock group, showed us pictures and press clippings he took out of an attaché case full of navigational maps. The others, all fluent in English, were all intent on discussing the differences between Mexicans and Americans. Mexican men touch easily and soon I'm being fondled, a hand on a leg or another too tightly around my shoulders. The more overt insinuations are directed at Peggy and Rose. One of the pilots jokes about an orgy, and then plans a weird game staging a mock marriage between Peggy and the tallest of the pilots. My role was the *padre* who would officiate at the ceremony. Another pilot began insisting that he should have the right to have Peggy first.

The bantering went on for another three quarters of an hour, the men still drinking one rum after another, the rooms very hot and full of smoke. The hotel was fancy, with a swimming pool in the lobby, but the rooms had no windows! Peggy seemed to be enjoying the marriage game, and perhaps she felt there was no other real way to relate. One pilot removed his shirt, complaining about the heat, but then encouraged the rest of us to remove ours as well.

Rose had a better understanding of the situation, and got Jaime to invite us all to a nightclub. He left with the two American women. Pleading work, I returned to the Pensione, feeling lucky enough to have escaped that sweltering room.

Love,
John

The Oaxaca Letters

11/10/74

Dear Mellon,

I've been reading D.H. Lawrence's sketches in *Mornings in Mexico* that Ross also loaned to me. Lawrence describes the Indian sensibility so sympathetically: it is governed, if that is the right word, by an "encircling timelessness" that is free of the obligations of the kind of measurement we take for granted. If they have money, for example, they want to spend it all immediately rather than having to worry about it. They lack our white passion for "invisible exactitudes," as Lawrence puts it. He seems fascinated by the Aztec theory that worlds are successively created and destroyed by convulsions of the sun. He writes that his house in Oaxaca was like a small fortress, all its windows on the street with thick bars. When he leaves his house, his "alien presence is like the sound of a drum in a courtyard," a feeling I can recognize here.

This morning Virginia and I squeezed into the bus to Tlacolula to visit its market. The town is twenty minutes outside of Oaxaca. The buses are beaten and decrepit, many seats are broken, and in the rear a belching vile, veil of black fumes. I took a jolting bus in Mexico City that felt like a lurching rollercoaster ride but this one went very deliberately across the flat brown plain. A bleating pig was tied to the roof, and it never stopped squealing. Sometimes, the pigs or chickens are inside the buses. The boy seated next to me sucked on sugar cane and spit the residue out of the open window; on the other side of the aisle, an Indian woman with a tiny baby that she displayed for her neighbor to admire with such sunny pride and joy.

First we visited its domed church where people were praying while we observed the gilded chapel studded with reflecting mirrors. The market itself is on a much smaller scale than Oaxaca's. Stalls of blazing color, some with cheap rayon dresses and embroidered blouses, piles of marigolds, purple lilacs, vegetables, coffee and cocoa beans, nuts and herbs. Women with long shawls and baskets on their heads, others selling food in pots hanging over round clay stones above coals. I tried some fried pigskin that tasted like bacon. Vendors were quite friendly, willing to let you sample. My beard precedes me and Virginia confessed she felt like Frieda Lawrence following D.H. Lawrence. His red beard astonished the Indians who believed it signified Christos returned.

Love,
John

11/11/74

Dear Mellon,

The mountains around Oaxaca are azure-blue at dusk while the clouds turn pink. First drops of rain, a dust-clearing downpour that lasted for an hour. Received a letter from Joyce saying that she hates to think of herself as my torturer. I guess I laid it on too thickly, but she must feel a bit guilty, and promises to attend to my material as soon as her spring books are ready for press. I'm taking it cheerfully, as a reprieve, a time to soak in sun, solace my soul. I feel rejuvenated here, protected so far in the "wheel of quivering meat conception" Kerouac alludes to in one of his *Mexico City Blues* poems. These poems, incidentally, which include his two wonderful elegies to Charlie Parker, have nothing to do with the city of Mexico but happen to have been written there in 1954.

 The Pensione Suiza is an ideal place despite its somewhat spartan style. My meals are served to me, my room gets cleaned daily, and Ross inevitably places a rose on my breakfast table. We chat in the morning over coffee, and I'm reading one of his books, a small university press publication called *Journey to Yanhuitlan,* an account of a trip to a monastery in 1948. His writing is as delicate and fragile as his gracious person, probably not destined for any large audience. Ross isn't hard-boiled like most journalists but more like the flowers he admires.

Yesterday morning, another outing with Virginia and Nicola, a new resident in the Pensione. She is thirty, calm, very self-contained, a voice like butter, with very little money. She was "impelled, driven" to come to Oaxaca. She seems like a lapsed candidate for a nunnery, radiant, but shielded by an impenetrable shell.

The town of Atzompa is quite close to Oaxaca, but two miles off the highway. The bus just waded through a rushing stream, bounced, pitched and weaved on a dirt road worse than any I've seen in Vermont.

In the town, we wandered into a music school with an instructor coaching seven boys playing brass instruments. They sounded comically awful though a lot like the band music I've heard blaring in the *Zócalo*. It reminded me instantly of Lawrence Ferlinghetti's take on the inevitable bands in *The Mexican Night*: "an enormous racket of trumpets and trombones and drums sounding as if some truck had just blown its muffler."

Then we visited three different potters all fabricating nativity scenes. When the black clay gets fired, it turns an earthen color. They live with families in adobe structures around a courtyard swarming with dogs, roosters, chickens, and a few huge, wallowing sows. Women were sorting beans, cooking potatoes, rubbing maize smooth with stones, kneading dough for tortillas. They had the round flat rocks used as ovens you described when you were in Surinam.

Walking through the quiet, dusty streets, I pass a flock of rams, burros bearing wood and baskets of black clay, high cacti walls, an hallucinogenic datura plant in one garden with its beckoning, large, orange flower, a yucca tree with white bell flowers, scarlet poinsettia, and magenta bougainvillea everywhere.

When we got back to Oaxaca, I spent a few hours in the market, this time with a notebook. A frenzy of activity: children carrying baskets of produce through crowded passages, men with pushcarts or dollies, women chopping ice or slapping dough, barkers shouting prices. There were blocks of vegetables, fruits, and flowers sold by stolid Indian women. Weavings were hung with ropes under canvas shade awnings, always five feet high, the average height of most humans here. Another area was devoted to leather goods, then clothing, yet another featured coral and shells. There was a section for agricultural tools and machetes, stands selling tacos or tortillas, cakes and cream puffs, fried fish, or pieces of chicken, pork or withered beef. There were herbs for many ailments from digestion to the devil, and men with tiny stands selling magical herbs. I watched one explaining the remedies provided by various pebble-shaped substances with evangelical fervor over his little altar of the Virgin Mary draped in beads and silver. I know I've written about this before, but I just can't get over the scale of the market and its gorgeous cascade of color.

What will happen when Mexico is developed into malls and supermarkets, and robots till the fields?

You should see it in a month and I'm excited. So much to show you here. One doesn't need anything fancy and I'm in jeans most of the time. You might bring a jacket and sweater since it may get cool in the evenings.

As ever,
John

The Oaxaca Letters

11/15/74

Dear Mellon,

After all these little excursions, I finally left Oaxaca for the road. Instead of working on the piece I started for the *Village Voice*, I went to San José del Pacifico. This is how it happened. Sunday night, in the *Zócalo*, I caught the eye of a young woman in a dirty blouse and a tattered long, many colored skirt at the next table. Dressed like an Indian, she somehow still seemed very American. She was sitting with a Mexican man who wore feathers on his vest and sombrero. He asked whether I would like to buy a flute, and I told him I had a friend—Juan—who had promised to make me one. Turned out pretty quickly that Raoul, the feathered man, was the member of Juan's extended "family" who had taught him to make and play the flute.

We were joined by a big, blond bearded young American. He had piercingly blue eyes and a broken front tooth. Except for a disconcerting facial twitch, he looked quite robust. An aspiring mathematician, Leaf had dropped out of Reed College in 1968. He had been on the hippie trail, picking fruit, joined the Rainbow Family for extended periods, and had lived in New Orleans and Austin where he knew Concha— the woman in the dirty blouse. I had recently spent weeks at the Humanities Research Center in Austin reading the Kerouac/Neal Cassady correspondence, so I was familiar with Sattva, the vegetarian restaurant, and the music spots they loved: Mother Earth, Armadillo, and Soap Creek where I had heard great bands like the locally famous Greasy Wheel. Leaf invited me to join his group returning to San José del Pacifico.

At noon, I met Leaf in the *Zócalo*, and Annie, a very overweight young woman from Los Angeles who was headed for Puerto Angel and would share gas expenses. She was living in Mexico on a couple of dollars a day until all her money was spent. It sounded like a familiar pattern. We had to hang around for a couple of hours, on Mexican time apparently, waiting for Raoul and Concha to complete necessary purchases.

We left at three singing songs in Leaf's filthy, crammed van. It fit right in with the many junkheap cars one sees everywhere in Mexico. The International Harvester had a hundred and sixty-five thousand miles on an odometer that no longer functioned, and it was on its second motor. The weather-beaten van had bald tires, leaked fluids, creaked and groaned, and belched black exhaust fumes you could smell inside. Leaf only had a temporary license and no registration, but he affirmed the van had been searched at every checkpoint with no difficulty. That seemed hard to believe, but this was Mexico.

After an hour on an immense, flat, brown plain, the road lined with sagebrush and twisted firs growing out of rocks, like semaphores of anguish, we stopped at a communal farm in the valley. La Vergel—the orchard—was owned by Margarita Dalto, a Mexican novelist who taught English in a primary school. Once the largest hacienda in the area, it was now mostly in ruins. Margarita served coffee on a patio facing the large courtyard. There were several parrots, one with a blue head that perched on my arm and drank from my cup. She showed us her fields, a new irrigation pump, and we picked some Swiss chard and anise. Then we were shown the house, inhabited by a few Americans who worked the farm for their keep. Before dusk, we returned to the fields to cut corn, fed the stalks to the cows after one of the Americans milked them, and skimmed off the cream for cheese.

At the house, about a dozen local farmers were meeting on the patio, trying to form a milk cooperative. We stayed in the kitchen, eating peanuts, and later rice and beans, tortillas, hot sauce, and tea. We were introduced to an American, Woody, who was plastering one of the rooms. He led us into another room with no furniture— holes in walls and ceiling but painted with suns, moons, and stars—and a concrete floor to sleep on.

At dawn, we were asked to go in the fields to help pick peanuts. A worker used oxen and a wooden plow to turn the ground and expose the roots. We picked until 10:30 when the sun became too hot, and had breakfast of toasted tortillas, black beans, the cheese made the night before, and black coffee.

The Oaxaca Letters

By noon we are back in the van. Two hours trying to listen to the crackling Mexican radio, fading in and out, the crazy broadcasts Ferlinghetti captures so perfectly in *The Mexican Night:* "...emitting a hilarious mixture of dramatic advertisements for shoes, American jazz played by violins and cornets, church bells thrown in to punctuate special announcements, sexy male announcers sounding as if they were simultaneously seducing a housewife, and reporting a fire in the studio, all mixed together with mariachis."

Approaching the mountains, the paved roads end and it is all bumps on dirt. The views are spectacular as we climb, little valleys, deep drops and gorges on the side of the road, small adobes with thatched roofs, reddish soil like parts of Colorado. At ten thousand feet, we reach the tiny town—a settlement really—of San José del Pacifico. It is situated in one of the little valleys with towering peaks above. There are spiny *cholla* trees and mescal cacti on the sides of the road. There was an inn where for a dollar one could sleep on a floor mat in a large shared room. Six hour drive to the west is Puerto Angel and the Pacific Ocean, and Annie decided to wait at the inn for the bus going there.

We stop in the one restaurant to have soup and tortillas. My chili rienza is too hot for me to eat. I am approached by an American man wearing a snappy white Panama hat who says he met me at the party at the Pensione Suiza for Juan and Nancy's departure. People seem to manifest here in a karmic mandala. He rolls several smokes and lights one. When I protest in amazement, he reassures me that there are no police in San José del Pacifico unless the army comes to search for revolutionaries. As if to prove this, he offers me peyote and tells me the town is a major mushroom center from the beginning of July until the early fall when the mushrooms can no longer be found.

Back in the van, we climb vertically on the roughest road I've ever seen, sudden deep pits and ridges worse than that one on the Navaho reservation where we broke the Austin's transmission. Remember that miracle when the Navaho mechanic crawled under the car and adjusted the transmission in ten minutes? How uncanny that his repair lasted for another two thousand miles until we reached our street in the West Village and the transmission died forever.

The van had enough clearance to go over big rocks, but it had to grind, claw, and wheeze its way up. Finally, Leaf parked on the edge of a sweeping curve. We walked for half an hour up another few thousand feet through a pine forest trail covered with dense foliage. Raoul was ahead, whooping calls to his "brothers" who descended to help transport the supplies the van conveyed. With the dozen flutes he sold in Oaxaca, Raoul had bought oats, rice, soy powder, fruits, and chocolate.

Finally, we descended a steep incline for ten minutes on a narrow, twisting deer trail to a secluded crescent in a V shaped valley clearing with three huts. Orange Indian paintbrush, blue lupins, purple thistles, marigold everywhere. Incredible vistas, no mechanical sounds, clouds impinging on the peaks above. We could not see the town below; only the sky and the trees around us.

The huts are fifteen feet long and ten feet wide, built of thin logs placed in a trench and lashed together. The floors are dirt and straw, the roofs are thatched with woven tall grass and corn stalks. In the hut we enter, there is a small wood cooking fire in one corner. There is no furniture except for shelves for books and dry goods. Outside, there is very pure water running on a bamboo track from above.

Five young men besides Raoul and Concha live in one of the other huts. One of them is Juan, who is preparing the food. Another, Andre, was French. This was the family with whom Juan and Nancy had lived; this was where she discovered she was pregnant, but now Juan seemed very silent and uncommunicative, almost sullen, perhaps recovering from catastrophe.

We would stay in this hut, communally used for meals and meetings. As the sun descended, there were prayers and benedictions led by Luis, who seemed to be the spiritual leader of the group. The worship mixed Christ culture with more cosmic and perhaps more ancient mushroom perspectives. We smoked some home grown very powerful marijuana, *sinsemilla*, giant

The Oaxaca Letters

buds of almost pure pollen. The higher the altitude, the more potent the product, I was informed. Then Juan served a dinner of soy soup and oatmeal with chunks of delicious, dark, homemade sweet bread. The dinner was simple, but filling enough, and we all shared a cracked brown jug of *pulque,* a fermented, milky drink with a sour, sudsy taste.

After dinner I got to speak French with Andre who has spent the past three months in this brotherhood. He has been on the road since the uprising of the French university students in Paris in 1968, an event, he claims, that was much more comprehensive and profound than the scattered events that occurred in the U.S. He lived for a year in Nepal where he learned to make flutes, then in India, then spent several years in the Andes. He knows the spine of the world, he tells me, the Himalayas and the Andes connected by a straight line through the center of the earth.

Soon, the men began to play their flutes and Leaf strummed the guitar. Luis told me he had been in university in Uruguay in 1968, and dropped out in his third year after being jailed for six months for his part in student protests. The key event for him had occurred ten days prior to opening of the Olympic Games in Mexico City in early October of 1968 when five hundred peacefully protesting citizens and university students at the Tlatelolco Plaza were murdered by special government troops.

Concha told me everyone in her group had retreated to the mountains as a result. They all ate mushrooms that they believed gave them a special sense of being in tune with the universe. When I asked about the possibility of being poisoned, she claimed that they could detect the right mushrooms by sight and smell. She said this with such sweet sincerity and I remembered Bonnie Bremser's comment in *For Love of Ray* that the Indian mushroom people "live each day as if their lives were gifts which they in turn dedicate to the mountain and the mushroom."

At some point, I do not know what time it was, everyone prepared for sleep. There was a mat for me to lie on and a thin blanket. The ground underneath felt hard and irregular, and I woke up after a few hours because the air on the floor seemed so cold. The air was dangerously thin and each exhalation formed a soft, misty puff. Was this what the Indians meant when they called themselves the "Cloud-People"? Crickets were humming despite the chill and it felt as if there was an activated energy field around us. I could see brilliant stars sparkling through crevices in the roof, and though it was cold, I felt something akin to the "Tropic of Cancer heaviness that held us all pinned to earth, where we belonged and tingled" that Kerouac described in *On the Road*.

As invigorating as it was there was something frightening about the experience as well. I knew I wasn't hearty enough to be anything more than a sojourner on the mountaintops, and that I would have to return soon or succumb to illness. In the early morning, the men washed in the cold water, an ice shower, and smoked some more. They fetched shovels, hoes, and machetes. Andre sharpened his machete with a stone, and led by Raoul they left to work in terraced garden plots without eating.

Juan escorted me up and then down the mountain to the dirt road. He had barely spoken a word to me, but was now confiding that Nancy intended to return to San Diego where she would have their child. He pointed the way to San José del Pacifico, not understanding, perhaps, despite my panting, that the lack of oxygen in the air and the exertion of climbing and descending were already too much for me. Juan seemed to shrug as I left and I believed it was the last time I would see him.

I passed burros carrying wood on my descent, and smiling Indians. When I reached the town, the bus arrived to convey me back to Oaxaca. Truncated as it was, I knew I had finally tasted adventure that was more visceral than vicarious. Multiplied by a hundred more such occasions, I thought, and one might end up with something like the overwhelming pell-mell pile up of all the searching journeys of *On the Road*. And if one could create the rhythmic surge that Kerouac brought to his sentences, you would have something worth admiring.

Love,
John

The Oaxaca Letters

11/16/74

Dear Mellon,

This morning I went to the dedication of a new dance stadium on the outskirts of the city. A dirt street leads up to Cerrin del Forte where one can see the entire city spread out in the valley below. Hundreds of schoolchildren, Boy Scout troops, kids in army fatigues. The town band for once sounded more or less in tune. The seven dances each celebrated another part of Oaxaca State. First, a group of a dozen women in long black braids with huge flower baskets on their heads who wore long white dresses that fanned out wide as they swirled. Then a dance of sixteen women in white embroidered dresses spreading shredded marigolds which gave way to three couples all in white with black sombreros, replaced by another group of couples with sashes. Then there was a dance with pineapples, the fruits flung into the crowd, another dance of two women in gorgeous fantail dresses, ending with the most floridly decorated group in papier-mâché outfits with bows and arrows. I left when the speeches began before the heat of the day.

Why don't you consider coming down here earlier? My hope is to leave Oaxaca for Guatemala by bus just after New Year. Try to travel light because it is a three-day bus ride.

Somehow, that swift flight into the mountains, into such a vastly different space, was jarring. Maybe that is an understatement; it was shocking, like space travel or an acid trip. The experience raises fundamental doubts and questions. Compared to the purity of life in San José del Pacifico, my past in New York seems so mired in routine and what now seem to be trivial concerns. Five of the six men I stayed with live without sexual contact and don't seem to care about much more than work, meditation, and the relief of holy smoke. I've been here for a few months now and realize how much I miss being with you—the warmth of my heart and the hearth of my life. You are the most loving person I have ever met, but our dynamic has been faulty and we alternate between radiance and strife.

Shouldn't our ambition be to create a more fluid concentricity whose exact center is our devotion to each other, making other ambitions and attachments a bit less important? Easy to write I know, but if we lose each other, we lose what is most worth having.

    So this is a Thanksgiving letter. We have so much to be thankful for—Perry Street, Vermont, our mutual talents, and health. I miss your presence, your bubbling enthusiasm, and hope to be with you soon!

Love,
John

11/18/74

Dear Mellon,

Yesterday was in French. At the *Zócalo* in the late afternoon I met an Algerian anthropologist and we spoke French for half an hour. Her pocketbook had been snatched and then recovered that morning, which she mentioned in an almost matter-of-fact manner. The market is known for having pickpockets who work in teams, one jostling while the other slices into a bag. She was waiting for two Canadian friends from Quebec whose truck had been broken into that morning, and when they showed up we went to the market to eat. I had a *tostado*, a toasted, flat open tortilla with shredded chicken and guacamole and sweetened, black coffee in a large soup bowl, scooped from a big vat. As

The Oaxaca Letters

long as it has been cooked, the food in the market is pretty safe, although dishes only seem to be rinsed in cold water.

This morning at breakfast Ross told me he just received the fourth rejection of his manuscript on D.H. Lawrence in Oaxaca. He seemed so calm and steady about his bad news. He just keeps plugging at his work, never seems down, a wonderful karmic illustration of fortitude and faith. His first book, he admitted, had been turned down by fifteen publishers before Crowell finally accepted it.

In the courtyard, Ross showed me a cacao tree with large glossy leaves. He opened a purple pod so I could see the cream-colored bean, the source of chocolate. Casually, he observed that I was becoming metamorphosed by Mexico, responding to the humanity in me that had been repressed by my own academic conditioning. I do feel less compulsive and less impatient, more able to accept doing nothing while waiting for Joyce's comments, just enjoying the bliss in being here now.

Astutely, and seemingly out of the blue, Ross also told me he thought I was less willing to deny sorrow in life. The tension and insecurity of my attempts to write are one source of potential pain, and your own history and disappointments can become a compounding factor. Maybe I'll be better able to accept suffering when it occurs, instead of trying to avoid it or escape. I do have to learn to be less governed by routine, moving the car when necessary, going to work at a certain time, eating meals on clock time. My compulsion to accomplish everything I wanted to encompass has resulted in the selfishness you spotted in our time of discord last spring. It is difficult to see one's own limitations, I suppose, but being so far away from the familiar can open a doorway to something new. My hope is that the ego that motivates me to write will diminish, making me more able to observe, to remove filters projected by the self.

One sign of change, perhaps, might be that I seem more able to write directly on my typewriter, and I'm trying to do the *Village Voice* piece in this fashion. That is the way Kerouac advised Ginsberg. Ross told me this was his training at newspapers, as reporters need to stress speed. Kerouac believed that immediacy lessens the possibility of conditioned self-censorship, writing to please an editor who wants a more conventional approach. I have always written my letters this way, words streaming out directly, with no opportunity to revise or respond to anything accept an intuitive outpouring. The result could be more honesty and fluidity.

    I worked in the terrace shade until Nicola began a conversation. She is in the ninth day of a purification fast. Maybe her intention is partly to save money as she lives on four dollars a day, and half of that is for her tiny closet of a room. When her money runs out, she will return to Kansas City and her waitressing job. She is a college graduate, an aware and sensitive person, but happy doing simple work. I realize you won't be able to come sooner because of your upcoming fashion job, but I hope Nicola is still here when you arrive because you will like her.

                                                    Love,
                                                   John

The Oaxaca Letters

11/20/74

Dear Mellon,

Ross took me to an opening for his friend, Bill Stewart, a painter who lives on Bleecker and Bowery. It was at the Alliance Française, and the paintings were quite vivid, displayed on an open patio. Wine and cheese, but a paltry turnout.

    Then Ross treated me to coffee and ice cream in the *Zócalo*. We had a good talk about Whitman. Suddenly I saw Woody, an especially animated carpenter with gleaming eyes whom I had met at La Vergel where he was restoring one of its rooms, and he joined us. He studied at Harvard when Leary was teaching there, one of the undergrads whom Leary turned on with acid. Woody followed Leary's prescription and had dropped out before completing his degree, and now lives in the mountains. He is fluent in Spanish—mine still staggers along—but when I asked him whether he felt it was safe, he said that on Halloween shots had been fired at his cabin. So alluring as Oaxaca is, rumors of danger haunt the *gringos*.

                                      Love,
                                      John

Beat Transnationalism

11/21/74

Dear Mellon,

Here is the awful aftermath of my trip to San José del Pacifico. Last night, as I was writing my account of that trip for the *Voice*, there was a knock on my door. It was Leaf, looking haggard and uneasy. Juan had given him my address.

The day after my departure his van had been vandalized, and his tires deflated. The spare tire and tools were gone. Foolishly, he decided to spend that night in his car. Before midnight, the van was surrounded by six men with machetes, one was waving a pistol and another had a rifle. A flashlight was directed at Leaf's eyes and the pistol was pressed to his temple. The men took his cash, passport, and visa, and then made him sign over all his traveler's checks. He suspects this may have happened because he had refused to pay a "mordida" for the protection of his vehicle. I let him sleep in my room, bought him breakfast in the market, gave him some money, and accompanied him to the bank this morning. He has other friends who will help him now.

Half an hour after leaving Leaf, in the *Zócalo,* I met a woman who warned that the governor of Oaxaca was about to leave his office. In the confusion over the change in administration, there could be a "sweep" of young Americans. She told me last week an American trying to buy marijuana was murdered in Mitla, and last night another one staying in her hotel was seduced on the same errand, beaten, robbed, and left outside in his shorts. Such reports, of course, frighten me and I think I will hole up in Suiza for a week.

"Oaxaca" has an alien, fierce, and almost sinister sound to my ear today—like Malcolm Lowry's ominous characterization of it in *Under the Volcano*: "The word was like a breaking heart, a sudden peal of stifled bells in a gale, the last syllables of one dying of thirst in the desert."

One consequence of foreign travel is an appreciation of how good it can be in the U.S. I remember how patriotic you were when you returned from Surinam and now I understand why. The whole episode with Leaf is quite upsetting because he could have modeled for one of Kerouac's happy-go-lucky what-the-hell characters in *On the Road.* Nicola is scared too and planning her return to Kansas City.

News like this is disappointing for you as you are preparing to come down here. As you probably realize from Surinam, South American traveling doesn't offer the same comfort zones as Europe. In Mexico, I fear, if an American has anything, some local may try to seize it. So while everything can seem as peaceful as it did seem to me with Juan's brothers so high in the clouds, there may be insidious dangers. I know I may be over sensitively paranoid about the street rumors I hear, but what happened to Leaf was real, and I was in his jalopy van a few days before. Isn't there a safe place left on this earth to visit without the welcome of *bandidos?*

Love,
John

11/24/74

Dear Mellon,

It has been getting cooler here, with a bite in the night air. I've been staying in the Pensione, having meals here, avoiding the *Zócalo* and the center of town, trying to complete the *Voice* piece. No word from Joyce Johnson yet, which is another source of anxiety.

Last night at dinner here, Michael Horne, an American actor who lives in Mexico City, shared another horror story of being jailed for four days on a marijuana set-up. William Burroughs told me last year that buying marijuana in Mexico was particularly dangerous for Americans because of informers who are paid for tips. In jail, Michael could not eat because the food was inedible; he cowered in a filthy cell afraid of rape. The cell had no window, its light was on constantly, its occupants had to sleep on the concrete floor and defecate there as well. When his family paid a ten thousand dollar fine, he was released.

He claimed every foreigner in Oaxaca was being watched. I do have a small amount of marijuana stashed in my room, but now I'm planning to bury it in the garden. Ross belittles my fears, but he works steadily and hardly leaves the Pensione. If he does, he often orders a taxi.

Love,
John

The Oaxaca Letters

11/29/74

Dear Mellon,

Sorry I haven't written, but I didn't even dare to walk to the *Zócalo* to mail a letter until the *Voice* piece was ready. I do wonder though whether it will be right for them: so many characters, so crowded with incident, maybe too far off their usual beat.

Yesterday was Thanksgiving and Nicola accompanied me to Xachila, and the monastery at Cuilapan. On the bus and at the market at Xachila, Nicola and I were the only apparent foreigners. We ate some raw sweet potato and turnip root, and tasted some *pulque*, then took another short bus ride to Cuilapan to see its sprawling sixteenth century monastery. The edifice was built with yellow sandstone, but some stones were light green, even pale lavender. Visited the bell tower, the monk's cold, silent cells, a large dining refectory. The place seemed practically deserted except for one grizzled, leering attendant who kept lurching after Nicola wherever she wandered. That was disquieting.

On the bus trip back to Oaxaca, only standing room and my head kept bumping against the low roof. Is it a sign that I no longer fit in Mexico? Back at the Pensione, Nicola, who has become a loyal friend, made me a tangerine juice drink and we ate a cucumber and avocado salad with miso and then grapefruits on the terrace in the hazy sunset. She has been very screwed up in the past, in analysis to learn her compulsive eating is a function of repressed sexuality. She is leaving soon and I hope she visits us in New York or Vermont.

I love you all the time and wonder whether my own past paranoia has prevented me from expressing it adequately? I hope your fashion shoot turns out successfully and I'm so happy that you will be here in a few weeks.

Love,
John

12/1/74

Dear Mellon,

Still no word from my editor. It may seem melodramatic or extremely impatient, but sometimes I resemble Sisyphus waiting for the mail to arrive or the hapless figures in Godot. All my haste to gather the materials I needed for my departure last summer only to have been sucked into this vacuum of unknowing.

A new temperature pattern here: hot when the sun is high, but quite cold in the night. The rooms are unheated and I use the three blankets in my room. I've gone to sleep at nine on several nights because of the chill.

My room now has some decoration other than the dull picture of a church and its bell tower that was here when I first occupied it. I've added some pine cones from San José del Pacifico, your Medicine Wheel card and your lovely photo of an apple in the snow, a snap of Juan, a postcard Kodiak Rose sent from Guatemala, Ross' drawing of a Japanese temple, a picture of Ginsberg from *Time Magazine*, and a poster advertising a Beat reading in San Francisco that Harold Norse sent me.

Ross, my literary cheerleader here, loaned me a copy of Lowry's *Dark is the Grave Wherein My Friend Is Laid* because it is set in Oaxaca, but much more maudlin, not nearly as fluent or compelling as *Under the Volcano*. It seems more like a preparatory notebook effort, about a drunk of gargantuan proportions (to use Lowry's description) on a pilgrimage to discover his past. With Lowry it is always a pilgrimage to hell. His character is a writer who is terribly afraid and makes his wife, Primrose, handle mundane matters he just can't face.

Also reading copies of past *New York Review of Books* that Ross has given to me. Despite my recent paranoia, Ross claims I look so much calmer than when I arrived with less tension showing on my face. Perhaps, naively, he doesn't realize the change he attributes to Oaxacan leisure is due to the sun. My tan hides a lot. He is leaving, also, on his way to visit kin in California, and I will miss him even though you might have found him too prissy and fastidious.

Reading is difficult right now because of a strike of automotive workers. The headquarters of Dodge, an American car company, are one street away and the strikers play amplified music while they picket from seven in the morning until late at night. It is disturbing and does intensify the noisy cacophony of the city.

I note your observation on the amount of detail in my letters. While they represent my Mexican experience, they are also letters to myself, a record, yes, but just as much a groping attempt to understand my baffled responses, unmoored somehow in unfamiliar surroundings. The letters have become my most important project right now, although they may be only for the future. The *Voice* piece has been largely drawn from them. I've been reading my carbons and I notice how I began beseeching you to come down sooner, only to swerve into warnings about incipient dangers I perceive for Americans in Mexico. Leaf's disaster followed by the actor's jail story were fulcrums, but except for the fearfulness those events caused, I've been in reasonably good health.

I suppose this paranoid turn is part of the karmic path too. My worries about your photographing in Mexico do have a real basis. It is really hard to hide your equipment on these streets where glaring poverty provides grim reminders of differences in fortune. My beard and long hair make me a "mark," to use Burroughs' expression, as your Nikons. Anyone with fair skin, as Lawrence puts it in *Mornings in Mexico,* is as apparent as "drums beating in a churchyard."

At the same time, a sort of convalescent on the sunny terrace of the Pensione Suiza, I feel content and relaxed. I don't even want to talk to Nicola who has begun yet another fast. I miss you and can't wait to see you. Eighteen days from now and you will be in Mexico City, and in a few weeks here with me. How lucky!

Love,
John

Beat Transnationalism

12/2/74

Dear Mellon,

For the last few days I've been reading Henry Miller's *Plexus*. It isn't nearly as compelling as the two *Tropics* novels he wrote in Paris in the thirties, and to some extent he may be repeating some of that material twenty years later. Some of it seems forced—the writer exercising his mental muscles to keep them limber—but it is still a great comedic ride for the reader, away from the subject of Mexico or the Beat Generation. At the same time, he is their immediate spiritual godfather.

He is describing his life in Brooklyn with his second wife, the speakeasy hustler who decides he should not get a conventional job so as to free him for his writing. She has these boyfriends and mysteriously always ends up with enough money to support Henry. His episodic tales are hilarious: boyhood escapades, selling mezzotints, watercolors, even candies in Village clubs, serving drinks in the speakeasy his wife ran just down the street where we now live. All the while he is sponging on his friends, eating gargantuan meals with them, playing pranks on them too. It is all burlesque and Tom Sawyer I guess, but what a relief from the chore of my unfinished manuscript.

In the evening, after my Miller escape, Nicola made us a few tortillas with onions, cucumber, avocado, miso, and tamari. She is planning to stay at La Vergel for a week, the commune I visited on the way to San José del Pacifico, and I will miss her occasional company.

Ross had told me earlier that there would be a giant fiesta that I should witness, and he offered to accompany me.

The *Zócalo* was more crowded than I'd ever seen it, lined with carnival games, food stands, a blaring band in each corner. There were dancers from Veracruz. We ate dough soaked in honey and then crashed our bowls to the ground for good luck. A physician friend of Ross' whose grandfather had been governor of Oaxaca when D.H. Lawrence lived here treated us to coffee and brandies, and then a drunken *paisano*, who had once been a guide for Ross, came over to hug him with great affection.

At ten, the fireworks began in the cathedral square, three towers made of reeds with circular spin-offs so the sparks showered immediately above our heads. As a finale, spurting fireworks launched from the balustrade of the cathedral, a happy Mexican crowd gasping in delight and amazement. The spectacle somehow helped dissipate my paranoia and I realized that the dourness of disposition I had noticed in the streets in my few recent outings was more a function of the cold spell than anything else.

Love,
John

12/3/74

Dear Mellon,

Spent another afternoon utterly absorbed in *Plexus*, spellbound by his tales of anarchic irresponsibility. I went to the *Zócalo* in the late afternoon to try to telephone, but couldn't quite face the prospect of your answering machine from such a distance. Also, I have so much to say I thought I would be on the phone too long. When we spoke last week you said that I spoke so slowly, and perhaps it was because the telephone seems alien to me right now: I haven't used one in months.

I've intended to call Joyce to find out what's up or down with my project, but have not been able to face that prospect either. Maybe I'm more like Lowry than Miller, stumbling over ordinary life and unable to fulfill its obligations. Miller at least persisted despite forty years of rejection before he found his audience.

    I wish you were here, though I understand you just can't rush off, that you need to plan and organize. Perhaps you could telephone me at the Pensione Sunday morning, on the fifteenth, so I can meet your plane. There is a flight that arrives at 8:30 in the morning, and a later one in the afternoon. I can't tell you how much I desire your warmth and love. I'm not lonely because there are many people around me in the Pensione but the center of my soul seems vacant without you.

                                                  Love,
                                                  John.

The Oaxaca Letters

12/4/74

Dear Mellon,

I wonder how you are feeling. I can't wait to show you some of what I've seen here. Wrote to several friends, but no replies. Is Mexico so far away? Is that why Joyce can dismiss me to the anxiety of uncertainty? This afternoon I tried to call her collect but the hotel phone was out—a telephone pole had collapsed on the corner. I walked to the post office but it was closed, and then another office with telephones where I was informed that I could not make an international call. Three strikes discouraged me.

After dinner, Ross asked whether I would accompany him to the *Zócalo* to hear a particular band, but when we arrived there was no music. We had a cappuccino and Ross proposed a walking tour of places I might not have seen so far. We started with a courtyard near the market that used to be part of a Jesuit monastery. Then we walked clear to the other end of town and saw the *Casa Cultural*, a former Capuchin nunnery, and the attached Church of the Seven Princes. Seven is a special number here and the state is divided into seven districts, each with its own special characteristics. Then we walked to La Merced, built in the seventeenth century and one of the oldest churches in town. It had a weird neon cross on its big dome and more neon in the courtyard. It seemed quite distasteful, garish, but Ross wanted to show it to me because local legend claimed its priest had paid himself for the restoration of the dome when it cracked after an earthquake, and perhaps to pay for it rented his own house to Lawrence when he lived here.

The real treat came next when we went to the opera house that had been built around the turn of the century. This, it turned out, was where the missing band was appearing. It made me wonder whether Ross didn't know this all along. The band accompanied a group of university students in a program of folkloric dances. The costumes were brilliant, especially for the plume dance.

Then to Casa de Cortez, a sixteenth century gothic building

constructed for Cortez though never occupied by him. The only occupants we saw were two shoemakers still at work at ten. On the way back to the Pensione, we stopped for a final cappuccino at the Hotel Francia where Lawrence stayed when he arrived in Oaxaca, and again just before his departure. Ross greets everyone he meets with a smiling *buenas noches*.

Strange aftermath of family dream, my parents living with me in Oaxaca, with my mother's father crying uncontrollably.

Love,
John

12/5/74

Dear Mellon,

It was so good of you to call me. I have been here for almost two months, and still waiting for Joyce's commentary. It seems an unbearable tribulation. Oaxaca now seems confining to me, and I am at a spiritual nadir. Take me to the man who has forgotten words so that I may converse with him.

I am now so unsure of what Joyce thinks of my manuscript, perhaps she sees it as just another cramped academic monograph fit only for burial on the shelves of a university library. Ross tries his best to take some of the load off me at mealtimes, but his concerns about my distress only seem to compound my restless anxiety.

I do want so much to show you a good time here. Can't wait to hold you in my arms.

                                                                    Love,
                                                                    John

                                                                    12/6/74

Dearest Mellon, my love,

I read your telegram—thank you so much for having lunch with Joyce. I feel enormous relief that you are arriving and that Joyce has not totally forgotten my project. I CAN'T WAIT TO SEE YOU!

Nicola has returned from her trip to La Vergel. She enjoyed working in the fields, but complained about intrigues and a coldness she felt from some of those living there, especially Margarita Dalto. This afternoon she told me she came to Oaxaca to recover from a six-month affair with the owner of the health food restaurant where she worked. Her employer has two children and initially Nicola had been involved with her employer's husband. Nicola is thirty, distrusts men, and thinks of sex in very puritanical terms.

We went to my favorite food stand near the *Zócalo* to have dinner and sat near the boiling fat where the tostadas and meat are dipped. Nicola stuffed herself as if to taste all the bad food in Mexico before she leaves. Although the Mexican diet can be awful, the atmosphere is so convivial. Returning to the *Zócalo*, we passed a *callenda*, a procession from the town of San Juan Tehuantepec of three trucks with little girls from five to ten years old all wearing white dresses. Some of them so poised they seemed like prima ballerinas or cherubim. Around the trucks were giant clowns in papier-mâché, some on stilts, some setting off firecrackers. There were women in regional costumes and the usual brass band.

Also got a letter from Hal, who is now going to Ecuador. He gave me the names of people in Panajachel who might help us find a place there.

Love,
John

The Oaxaca Letters

12/8/74

Dear Mellon,

Yesterday morning Juan appeared. He had been my conduit to the holy smoke and its possible epiphanies, but now he seemed soiled. He accompanied Nicola and me to the market for breakfast and on the way he pointed to a rainbow in a fountain, just the sort of magical spark he would notice and admire. Nicola seemed immediately drawn to Juan and he so attentive to her. Later we sat in a café on the *Zócalo,* and I asked Juan to make me a flute for you.

His appearance distresses me somehow, and I wonder whether my karma is to cool out now, to attach less significance to transient relationships. Every few minutes another of Juan's friends would stop to greet him. Woody, the Harvard carpenter from La Vergel, was one of them; another, a seedy American with a very weathered face, gave me and Nicola some peyote.

The atmosphere in the streets was unusually tense. The town buses were being used as barricades to prevent another demonstration of the automotive workers. I was relieved to hear that Juan was waiting to return to San José del Pacifico. As if to escape the blaring loudspeakers of the strikers, Nicola surprised me by deciding to go with him. Mexico must be conducive for impulsive decisions.

Love,
John

12/9/74

Dear Mellon,

This morning, I received Joyce's comments and suggestions. She thought what I did to revise the Ginsberg section resulted in a major improvement. This is very encouraging, though I never imagined writing a book would require so much planning, time, and effort. I hope it will be worth it in the end.

    I loved your long letter that arrived at the same time. What you say about our blue auras is interesting, and how we turn red as we regress to childishness, how we sometimes have been like two children holding on to each other in the dark, or other times playing gaily in the light.

    I am so happy we will be together in a week. I hope it will be for a long, long time.

                                                   Love,
                                                   John

The Oaxaca Letters

12/10/11

Dear Mellon,

I don't know whether you will receive this letter though I'll share the carbon with you when you arrive. Worked on my Kerouac material most of the day. I did receive a surprising telephone call though. It was Nancy Silverman calling from Mexico City because she had not heard from Juan for weeks. She cried several times during the conversation. They had been legally married in Veracruz, and immediately afterwards Juan became uncooperative and despondent. She believes Juan started to take Librium, which can be obtained without a prescription in Mexico City, when his visa was denied. A consular official in the American Embassy had suggested he cut his hair because so many Mexican men married American women to get into the U.S. Juan suggested they could return to his brothers in San José del Pacifico, but Nancy saw that didn't seem feasible with an infant. Previously, Juan had been so responsive to anyone else's needs; now, he showed a calloused indifference to hers. One day when she was at work, Juan took all the money she had saved working as a typist, and just abandoned her.

    The idea to have a child, she claimed, had been Juan's, and her intention from the start had been to help him. I advised her to return to San Diego, that it would not be safe for her to have a child if she was indigent in Mexico. I did not tell her—because it was too heavy—that this meant she would lose Juan forever, although I suspect he was her fantasy from the moment she met him. He was only twenty; he had been in and out of reform schools as a child she now told me. Nicola had shown me only two days earlier how attractive to American women Juan could be.

    Nancy's story revealed the extent to which I had romanticized Juan as the returning Mayan, perhaps a little like the way Kerouac saw Terry, his Mexican migrant lover in *On the Road*. Had I denied my more circumspect and cautious instincts to be so charmed by Juan because of his difference, not his talent or intelligence? Juan represented the exotic stranger, the figure in D.H. Lawrence or Kerouac whose appeal is based on the elemental, the simplified, what seems the pure opposite of western conditioning—but was it merely decadent to succumb?

Love,   John

12/13/74

Dear Mellon,

It is the day of the wanderer's return. In the morning, as I was writing a new introduction to my Kerouac section, Leaf knocked on my door. He was filthy, his hair matted, his jeans ripped, his backpack had only one frayed strap. He told me he never got his van back but sold it for a song, and he had a garbled tale of being robbed again by what he referred to as the gestapo in San Jose. He was hitchhiking to Mexico City in a few days, the archetypical road-hippie offspring of the Beat Generation. I gave him another fifty pesos for the road.

    Nicola returned in the late afternoon from her tryst in the mountains. She admitted she instantly had been irresistibly attracted to Juan. They spent one night in a cubicle in the inn in

The Oaxaca Letters

San José del Pacifico. The following morning, Juan took what he had purchased in Oaxaca, and left her in the inn, returning to Raoul, Luis, and the others at the top of the mountain. She was stunned when she realized she had been deserted after a single night. Now, she said almost in a whimper, she was again thinking of her return to Kansas City.

> Love and see you soon!

Diary Notations:

12/16/74

I fasted yesterday, only drinking two glasses of water. Early this morning I chewed the bitter, dried peyote buds—called "buttons"—that Juan gave me last week. Ginsberg wrote the "Moloch" section of "Howl" after peyote and Native Americans all over the continent have been ingesting the bitter juices of the plant for centuries as part of their ritual observance. Peyote can induce dangerous regurgitation that can distort, confuse, or delay any hallucinogenic effect. In *Junky*, Burroughs describes a convulsive spasm ten minutes after chewing a dose of peyote and a clogged feeling like a hairball stuck in his throat. In a dream later that night, he imagined himself turning into a plant that becomes another central metaphor in *Naked Lunch*.

To avoid the potential physical distress associated with peyote, Juan had instructed me to fast. I thought the trip might be a way to prepare emotionally for your arrival, a path to stripping down the psyche.

Waiting on the terrace in the sun for the effects to begin, Ross came over with his usual platitudes on revision; sometimes his remarks are so conventional, a little like Polonius preaching the commonplace and obvious. He is reading Anais Nin's diaries that he finds posturing and vain. He loaned me a copy of Lady Cynthia Asquith's diaries for comparison and a B. Traven Mexican thriller.

I began to feel a sensation of floating a half hour later in the market. Sitting in the sun, I watched the food vendors setting up their stands, and other workers setting up booths for the Christmas carnival. No nausea but no desire for food. Walked very slowly up Independencia, perhaps for the first time here responding to the rhythm of the place. The colors of the fruits and vegetables seemed so intense, and textures had a vitality I had never felt before, the smells of flowers and fruits, the fermenting odors of bananas and peaches in the heat had an unprecedented pungency. I glided on marveling for several hours for block after block able, I thought, to comprehend—as confused as Kerouac who had the same empathetic identification—the fragments of Spanish or *Quetzal* I overheard.

I felt entirely safe, buoyant in my illusion and in my admiration for the bustling harmony around me. Indian families crouched on their haunches eating tortillas in the streets, children still asleep on doorsteps. The delicious smell of bushes and mosses being sold by elderly women as Christmas decorations. Although my personal circumstances were entirely different, the sheer radiance of the market that morning and its warmth reminded me of a similar spectacle of brilliance—despite the surrounding poverty—in Kerouac's Mexican novel, *Tristessa*.

The Oaxaca Letters

Too weak to continue walking, I spent the next few hours on a sunny bench in the *Zócalo*. Met one of the young men from Raoul's band in San José del Pacifico who was selling two kilos of weed. Was that what they were growing then? Met a young American in shorts on his way south to purchase hardwood for knives, another American couple who wanted to buy mushrooms. Suddenly, there was Juan with the flute in a rope bag for you. But it wasn't quite a gift; he wanted 100 pesos to get to San Christobel de las Casas.

In the great Cathedral, a special communion mass was being observed, a priest drinking from a silver chalice, an organist playing on the edge of the congregation. I'm thinking of your imminent arrival, praying for your well-being and our mutual capacity for understanding.

12/28/74

The longer I remained in Mexico, the more I began to appreciate its dangers, the sinister edge of which is so present in *Junky*. Mellon joined me before Christmas, on assignment from *The Magazine of Natural History* to photograph the Indians of the Oaxaca Valley, their irrigation system and flower cultivation. She contacted the Oaxacan Water Authority which provided a car and driver. We spent a week visiting colonial irrigation systems until one evening at dusk we stopped in a remote, isolated area so that Mellon could photograph a modern dam. From out of nowhere, two armed men approached the car and asked our driver whether the *gringos* wanted marijuana. We returned to the car immediately and our driver took off, convinced the men were *banditos*. They took a few shots at us, too, as the departing car careened through a dry riverbed at high speed. We were all bounced around a bit, safe enough, though terrified.

On Christmas Eve, we attended a midnight mass at the main Cathedral with the two domed bell towers. We were there less as celebrants than to absorb the pomp and ceremony, imbued by the sense of devotion and sanctity. Afterwards, drinking some *Manzanilla* tea in a *Zócalo* café, I asked Mellon why she had answered so few of my letters.

She told me as harrowing a tale as any I had yet heard in Oaxaca. Doing fashion and rock photography in New York, she had hired a new assistant, Kolek, a young Polish émigré. The son of a prominent photographer and filmmaker in Warsaw, Kolek was pressured by the police to spy and then inform on his father's suspected anti-communist activities. Kolek was talented and ambitious, but also impetuous and flamboyant. When he got a job on a crew filming in northern Mexico, he absconded, and crossed the border requesting political asylum. In New York he was accommodated by a sports journalist whose wife was a Polish actress and wanted to help.

Near the end of October, Mellon decided to visit our old farmhouse in Vermont. We had a small Ford Pinto wagon with an engine that had been built in West Germany, two years old, which I had left in her care. Suddenly, driving up the Taconic Parkway, Kolek exclaimed "This is how you women drive," seized the wheel and turned it sharply, causing the car to fly off the highway at sixty mph and crash into a tree.

Dazed, Mellon got out, miraculously only with a cut on her forehead that bled profusely, but Kolek was badly hurt. The car had hit a tree at over sixty miles an hour and flipped over. In shock, Mellon started to photograph the scene. A nun stopped her car and cradled Kolek's head in her arms until the ambulance and the state trooper arrived. The trooper wanted to arrest Kolek for interfering with the operation of a vehicle, but Mellon convinced him not to arrest him.

Kolek's request for asylum had been denied. Desperate to avoid deportation, he had attempted this suicidal act as a means of remaining in the U.S.A. The smashed car was towed to Mellenville, New York. When Mellon visited Kolek in intensive care, he was in traction and heavily bandaged. What struck her was another coincidence—the bandages covering his forehead were imprinted with the label "Warsaw, Indiana."

1/15/75

The carnival in Oaxaca lasted until the New Year. One night, Mellon decided she wanted to ride the whip, a circling mechanical wheel pitched at a forty-five degree angle with individually rotating open cabins. We never noticed all the Mexicans exiting. When we were the final occupants, the only *gringos* left, the wheel began to accelerate and our cabin to swirl so rapidly that we gripped the restraining bar and screamed. Our heads seemed ready to fly off but the Mexican operators would not stop it. Was this the final stop of the "the wheel of quivering meat conception" that Kerouac alludes to in an enigmatic poem about death in *Mexico City Blues* or a spontaneous expression of anti-American prejudice? We were so shaken by the incident that we decided to leave Oaxaca.

I was afraid to drive in Mexico so we took the bus south to San Christobal de las Casas, a town eight thousand feet high, populated primarily by people of Indian descent who dress in the old manner, in bright red and black elaborately embroidered garments. During all my time in Mexico, I had remained healthy by drinking bottled water or beer and avoiding anything uncooked, but I arrived in San Christobal with a serious case of *tourista*—the dreaded runs. Weakened, I took Lomotil, which contains an opiate, and stayed in bed for a day.

The next day was gloriously sunny, hot and dry. Around

midday I felt dehydrated and wanted some clear, hot soup. On our way to a restaurant, we met Juan, who said he was now living close by. He led us down an alley to an opening between three small cabins. A group of his friends were seated outside on the ground in a circle. Someone gave me a wooden folding stool and passed me a joint that I foolishly inhaled. I was happy to see Juan again and feeling stronger because we had unexpectedly reconnected.

Mellon remembers that I turned white and swooned into her arms. She cried for help. An old woman brought brandy and forced it between my parched lips. For an indeterminate period of time, I felt as if I was watching the group from twenty feet above, with most of Juan's companions conversing as if nothing had occurred.

Extremely agitated, Mellon bent over my body, desperately trying to revive me. My impression is that I had somehow detached, content to be observing from above, drawn back only by the extent of Mellon's grief. Whether this was an out-of-body experience, a fainting spell or a hallucination, my collapse depended on the combination of Lomotil, a lack of liquid in the hot sun, the altitude, and the puff of marijuana.

I had been reading Carlos Castaneda's Don Juan books, the marvelous mixture of sorcery and anthropology, and I interpreted this final meeting with Juan as a warning to leave Mexico.

1/25/75

On New Year's Day of 1975, Mellon and I took a crowded bus south to Guatemala. Unlike the modern bus that had brought me to Oaxaca from Mexico City, this bus had been built before World War Two, and its suspension was shot. It was full of diesel fumes and crammed with market produce and cardboard boxes on its

The Oaxaca Letters

roof, fastened with ropes. Struggling goats and pigs were tied to that hot roof too. All the other passengers were Indian, many of them carrying children or bamboo cases containing chickens. Some of them were on a religious pilgrimage, squeezing up and down the narrow aisle with a large wooden crucifix, singing psalms while the bus lurched around precipitous mountain curves.

The bus arrived in Panajachel on Lake Atitlán, a large body of water framed by three volcanoes. Panajachel was our destination, known on the hippie trail through South America for its dramatic beauty. As soon as we descended we saw Kodiak Rose seated at a curb, smiling as if she were expecting us as part of some Magical Mystery Tour. It was serendipity but it also seemed like a manifestation of the kind of lasting communion that had sustained Kerouac and Ginsberg. Surely enough, Rose found us a room to rent in Peggy's house on the water where we spent a recuperative month, sleeping on a thin mattress on the floor in a wool blanket, decorated with Quetzals, cooking fresh fish from the lake, and gorging on enormous saffron-colored papayas. Sometimes, we ate at the Hamburguesa, a restaurant crowded with Americans on the road where we could satisfy ourselves very inexpensively. We swam in the lake and rowed across in a communal longboat to visit the Indian villages. Life seemed simple and sweet, and I finished the work on *Naked Angels*.

Though not as sinister as Mexico, Guatemala was not without its dangerous edges. Ross had advised me—he was a former newsman—that insurrectionary activities were brewing in Oaxaca and there were others even more fully developed in Guatemala, El Salvador, and Nicaragua. Once, when I entered a bank to cash a traveler's check in nearby Solalá, a tense soldier jammed his rifle into my throat and forced me to the floor. My full beard made him assume I was a terrorist.

Instead, I was subjected to an intense instance of terror. The name Solalá was disarming, diminutive almost, but from that moment it signified "goodbye" for me.

By the end of January, I had to return to teaching. My

manuscript was completed. On its last page, I had scrawled a note to myself, quoting from Lawrence Ferlinghetti's *The Mexican Night:* "He who travels on peninsulas must expect someday to turn back."

III
The Triumvirate:
Ginsberg, Kerouac, Burroughs

An Emotional Time Bomb:
Allen Ginsberg's "Howl" @ 60

> "A sound poetic training is nothing less than the science of being discontented."
>
> Ezra Pound

I. A Subterranean Celebration

Allen Ginsberg's poem "Howl" was the most controversial and influential long poem written by an American during the second half of the twentieth century. "Howl" was written in San Francisco in 1955, when Ginsberg was twenty-nine years old. It might be seen as a manifesto announcing the appearance of a new generation.

Previously, as an undergraduate at Columbia University he had edited the literary review and won the encouragement of poet and professor, Mark Van Doren, for his polished imitations of sixteenth- and seventeenth-century British poets. When he graduated in 1947, he returned to his hometown of Paterson, New Jersey and began an informal tutorial with the poet William Carlos Williams, whose pediatric practice was in Paterson. Ginsberg had already made a powerful impression on the older poet with two remarkably eloquent letters he had sent to Williams, accompanying some of his early work. Williams was so intrigued by the letters that he would include them in his epic poem, *Paterson*. The friendship that ensued was mutually beneficial as Williams' vernacular sense of natural expression helped deflate a stilted and romantic literary self-consciousness in Ginsberg's early work.

Nevertheless, in the early 1950s, Ginsberg was unknown, unpublished, and completely unable to find any audience for his work. In 1950, his *Book of Doldrums*, a collection of early poems, had been rejected by Robert Giroux, the prescient young editor who had already published Jack Kerouac's first novel. In 1952, Random House rejected another early collection, *Empty Mirror*, despite its generous introduction by Williams.

Dejected by his lack of success, feeling that as a poet he had only managed to become "a ventriloquist of other voices," Ginsberg followed his friends William Burroughs and Jack Kerouac to Mexico. Living on a plantation in Chiapas, Mexico became a transformative experience, opening a doorway to the discovery of an authentic new voice. "Howl" was to be its first expression.

The poem was written for an occasion. Ginsberg had moved to San Francisco, where he had met a circle of young poets, including Gary Snyder and Michael McClure. Late in the summer of 1955, a group of young poets and painters were gathering for philosophical discussions on Sunday mornings at the home of Kenneth Rexroth, an older poet, a classicist, translator, and unofficial leader of a group of San Francisco anarchists. Rexroth asked a painter named Wally Hedrick to organize a group poetry reading. Hedrick helped direct an experimental art gallery on Fillmore Street in San Francisco, a run-down area. Previously, the location had served as an auto mechanic's repair shop and it still had a dirt floor. The Six Gallery had only had one show—the work of a figurative, little known painter named Richard Diebenkorn. In his book, *Scratching the Beat Surface,* Michael McClure remembered a large square area at the rear of the gallery with a display of "orange crates swathed in muslin which had been dipped in plaster of Paris to make splintered, sweeping shapes like pieces of surrealist sculpture."

The Triumvirate

Ginsberg was eager to participate in the group reading, and he typed dozens of postal invitations to what he promised would be "a charming event" conducted by a "collection of angels." In a remarkable book annotating his own poem, *Howl: the Original Draft Facsimile*, Ginsberg has maintained that what he wrote in the last week of August, 1955, was in part a compensation for his own "worldly defeat" and not intended for publication:

> I sat idly at my desk by the first-floor window facing Montgomery Street's slope to gay Broadway—only a few blocks from City Lights literary paperback bookshop. I had a secondhand typewriter, some cheap scratch paper. I began typing, not with the idea of writing a formal poem, but stating my imaginative sympathies, whatever they were worth. As my loves were impractical and my thoughts relatively unworldly, I had nothing to gain, only the pleasure of enjoying on paper those sympathies most intimate to myself and most awkward in the great world of family, formal education, business and current literature.

When the reading occurred on October 7th, a Friday evening, there was a turnout of over one hundred people. Ginsberg's friend, Jack Kerouac, was in the audience and, as he later recalled in *The Dharma Bums*, collected dimes and quarters from what he characterized as a stiff audience for three gallon jugs of California Burgundy. These jugs circulated around the room as the poets and audience members imbibed.

Rexroth introduced each of the young poets. Philip Lamantia, a local surrealist, read the poems of the late John Hoffman, who had died in Mexico. He was followed by McClure, the youngest member of the group, then Philip Whalen, Ginsberg, and finally Gary Snyder. Ginsberg, in a worn navy sweater and Levis, only read the first hundred strophes of the poem, its first part where he enumerated the adventures and catastrophes of certain members of his own "mad generation," because that was all he had then completed to his satisfaction. Ginsberg's reading, ending in his own tears, was a fifteen-minute rhapsodic performance. He would continue to read the poem up and down the West Coast, adding the second and third sections, and finally the "Footnote to 'Howl'" as these sections were completed.

Michael McClure saw the initial reading of "Howl" as a point of no return for American poetry. He realized that no American poet had been as outspoken as Ginsberg had in "Howl," that it was as if "a barrier had been broken, a human voice and body had been hurled against the harsh wall of America." For Gary Snyder the event was a "subterranean celebration." He walked away after the initial reading, remarking "'Poetry will never be the same. This is going to change everything.' Everyone who attended was set back. It was the power of 'Howl' and the defining moment in all our literary careers." Martha Rexroth, Kenneth Rexroth's much younger wife, asked Ginsberg for a copy of what he had read. With poet Robert Creeley, she typed a stencil and mimeographed twenty-five copies, a *samizdat* beginning for the poem.

Another member of that initial audience, poet and small-press publisher, Lawrence Ferlinghetti, sent Ginsberg a telegram the next day, beginning by paraphrasing Emerson's letter to Whitman after the sage had read "Song of Myself": "I greet you at the beginning of a great career." Impatiently, Ferlinghetti's next line was "When can I get the manuscript." Ferlinghetti's ambition was to print poetry in an inexpensive paper format. To save money, he had the first two thousand copies printed in England. These were transported by sea but seized by San Francisco Customs, leading to a trial, vindication, and an enormous audience formed by the attempt to censor the poem.

II. A Call to Power

> When I reflect that the task which the artist implicitly sets himself is to overthrow existing values, to make of the chaos about him an order which is his own, to sow strife and ferment so that by the *emotional release* those who are dead may be restored to life, then it is that I run with joy to the great and imperfect ones, their confusion nourishes me, their stuttering is like divine music to my ears.
>
> Henry Miller, *Tropic of Cancer*

No poem in our recent history has had more impact on the culture it confronts than Allen Ginsberg's "Howl." As Richard Eberhart put it in a piece in *The New York Times Book Review* in 1956, after the publication of *Howl and Other Poems,* "This poem has created a furor of praise or abuse whenever read or heard."

Yet nothing usually called poetry—think of Robert Frost's metrically comforting "Stopping By Woods on a Snowy Evening"—resembles the rushing propulsion of "Howl." Unlike Frost's more contained, reflective meditation, "Howl" announces itself like a declaration or a manifesto, and Ginsberg's history of his own generation is a panegyric of ebullience and despair.

Traditionally, most of the modern poems we read focus on some particular memory or event, concentrating with visual certainty on a finite, measurable experience—think of the clarity of William Carlos Williams' "The Red Wheelbarrow," or of Ezra Pound's haiku-like "Alba," the close relation of its lovers projected by the image of the pale, wet leaves of the lily-of-the-valley on the surface of the water in the dawn. With its long lines crossing the expected boundaries between poetry and prose, "Howl" is so much more overwhelming in its relentless barrage of detail, so much more panoramic in its scope, so much more transformative in its ambition. As Emerson first maintained in the talk on poetry that so galvanized Walt Whitman, the experience of each new age requires a new form of confession.

In 1981, covering the 25th anniversary reading of "Howl" at Columbia University for *The Soho News,* a downtown New York newspaper, I heard poet Anne Waldman describe Ginsberg's epic history of his own contemporaries as a "monumental hymn to the liberation of the American spirit from postwar material-industrial paranoid doldrums and hypocritical self-imposed mind and body restraints. It is a poem of desperate dejection purged and epiphanied through outrageous confession and celebration." The key word in Waldman's remark is "hymn," although it may seem an unusual choice given the unprecedented candor and the vaulting, ranting, almost hysterical anger that energizes Ginsberg's poem. The igniting rage of the poem is felt in its often-cited first lines, paradoxically introducing the "best minds" of his generation "destroyed by madness, starving, hysterical, naked," dragging themselves through African-American ghettoes looking for drugs.

"Howl" presents the record of the suffering and magnanimity compounding the experiences of a marginal group of outsiders during the particularly repressive period of the 1950s. They were a small part of what was considered a "Silent Generation," although Ginsberg vociferously raises the volume of their pain to an almost Artaudian level. As he noted in *Journals: Mid-Fifties*, at the time he was writing "Howl," "We have not yet had a crystallization of real grief in a poem since imagism."

Kerouac had called such expressions the "unspeakable visions of the individual," one of a list of principles that Ginsberg had posted on his headboard in San Francisco when he was writing "Howl." Ginsberg's ability to candidly commit to the unspeakable led to the spectacular outpouring of feeling that distinguished "Howl," a counter to the silence of a generation and the understated decorum of many of the poets in post-war America.

The poem works as a sort of *roman à clef*, based on the sensational, and sometimes exaggerated, exploits of the poet's own companions. For example, survivors like Tuli Kupferberg, who jumped off the Brooklyn Bridge in an unsuccessful suicide attempt, or Carl Solomon, who threw potato salad at a lecturer on Dadaism and who subsequently spent years in mental institutions. With a driven, insistent logic, each new figure committing another absurd and dramatic act is introduced with the pronoun "who," an exhaled sound of haunted lamentation, exhaustion, and woe.

Over a century earlier, Emerson had predicted that American literature would become more autobiographical. At one point, near the end of the poem, Ginsberg even offers the actual names of some of his closest friends—a nucleus of the Beat group—Peter Orlovsky, Lucien Carr, Herbert Huncke, Jack Kerouac, William Burroughs, and Neal Cassady, "secret hero of these poems." The list is a mock- Homeric recitation of defeated warriors, although, at least in the eyes of conventional publishing, the use of actual names of living people might have seemed libelous. It certainly was unprecedented.

The annotated facsimile edition of *Howl* shows how so many of the lines in the poem can be traced to events in Ginsberg's life, however distorted: he had been "expelled from the academies for crazy & publishing obscene odes on the windows of the skull," his friend Huncke had "walked all night with shoes full of blood," his friends Judith Malina and Julian Beck of The Living Theatre had distributed "Supercommunist pamphlets in Union Square weeping and undressing."

The gestural signals in the first section of the poem, weeping and undressing, jumping off bridges, walking in bloody shoes, being expelled from a university, and gothic images like the windows of the skull are part of the garish glare of lives presented on an extreme edge. The anger is magnified by lines like, "with dreams, with drugs, with waking nightmares, alcohol and cock and endless balls" or the more blatantly explosive "fucked in the ass by saintly motorcyclists." If in "Song of Myself" Whitman struggled to overcome the "howls restrained by decorum" by indirection and insinuation, Ginsberg was clearly without such compunctions and flagrantly displayed his contempt for the censorious restraints of convention.

Instead of the apathy associated with the 1950s, Ginsberg's "mad generation" is characterized by its desperate hyperactivity, a hipster avant-garde who eats fire, slashes wrists, drinks turpentine, burns cigarette holes in their arms, "who plunge themselves under meat trucks, looking for an egg," who jump "off fire escapes off windowsills off Empire State out of the moon," who scribble "all night rocking and rolling over lofty incantations," disappear into Mexican volcanoes, or journey obsessively to satisfy some visionary yearning. Such details are presented as a flowing catalogue of casualty, comedy, and celebration. The touches of incongruity—"investigating the F.B.I. in beards and shorts with big pacifist eyes . . ." that filter through the poem often seem bewildering. The hyperbolic fusion of anguish and release that animate this part of the poem help register the excess that provides the adrenaline rush that characterizes "Howl." Each new detail contributes to a cumulative formula for "the madman bum and angel beat in Time" at the end of part one, who serves as Ginsberg's code hero.

However, this stream of images, which to uninitiated readers sometimes seemed endless, provoked the immediate objections to Ginsberg's poem. "Howl" was as much a confrontation of Victorian propriety as Henry Miller's *Tropic of Cancer* with its ambition to cause a "resurrection of the emotions"—Miller's novel had appeared in Paris in 1934 but was still unpublishable in the United States in 1955 when Ginsberg wrote his poem.

"Hold back the edges of your gowns, Ladies, we are going through hell," Ginsberg's mentor, William Carlos Williams, perceptively noted in his brief preface to *Howl and Other Poems*. Ginsberg's "emotional time bomb," as he put it in the facsimile *Howl*, with its "nitroglycerine shrieks" and its demands for instant lobotomy would shock universally, as suggested by John Hollander, a former Columbia classmate who reviewed the poem in *Partisan Review,* deploring Ginsberg's "dreadful little volume" which only displayed "an utter lack of decorum of any kind." Hollander's dismissive remark quite accurately understood the initial rejection of the poem by the genteel establishment that controlled American poetry in the 1950s. Ginsberg poem was an awful breach, a scandalous violation of the accepted order and propriety, so no wonder its publication could only be sanctioned by judicial process.

An interpretive response to Whitman's first long poem, "Song of Myself," a much more contemplative poem written almost exactly a century earlier, "Howl" moves with the sudden impact of an avalanche, perhaps because it is much shorter. Like Whitman, "showing more always and with velocity," Ginsberg's rhythmic repetition and use of the participial case urges the movement forward: his lost battalion of Platonic conversationalists "rocking and rolling in the midnight solitude," lighting cigarettes in racketing "boxcars boxcars boxcars" or "yaketayakking screaming vomiting whispering facts . . ." with a speed the politeness of commas could only stall.

More than its narrative—perplexed as it is by enigmatic, telescoped juxtapositions like "hydrogen jukebox," "angelic bombs," or the "lamb stew of the imagination" —it is the rhythmic sweep of Ginsberg's poem that propels the reader along a surging continuum. It would take him over twenty minutes to read the entire poem and its leaping momentum is in part also a function of the potential of the long line, a line as long as his breath would permit, resulting in an expression that was as much performative as printed on a page.

Ginsberg manipulates the rhythm and it shifts in the second part of the poem, the Moloch section, to a more staccato terror punctuated by exclamation marks signifying horror, a total of eighty-eight of them employed in the fifteen strophes of the section. The pounding beat of those exclamation marks induces the fear of Moloch, "the heavy judger of men," whom the biblical Ammonites would propitiate with the sacrifice of their children.

Replacing Whitman's almost pantheistic love of nature, Moloch becomes the metropolitan deity of Baudelaire's "unreal city" drawn by Ginsberg with Orwellian overtones. Infused with Pound's hatred of the usury implicit in the western money system, Ginsberg's Moloch has a "soul of electricity and banks," blood of running money, and loves "endless oil and stone!" For Ginsberg, the corporate-military complex, and the careerism and consumerism it uses as inducements for the suspension of human values, is exactly what his "best minds" are desperate or brave enough to reject. Parts one and two of the poem violently demonstrate how Ginsberg's generation is martyred on the crucible of convention and materialism. His sympathy is clearly with those whom he sees as victims: "children screaming under stairways."

The tone changes as the third part of the poem narrows the focus on Carl Solomon, the friend Ginsberg met in Columbia Psychiatric Hospital in 1947, to whom the poem is dedicated. In a profound psychic sense, Carl is a displacement of Naomi Ginsberg and the prolonged grief her son felt after her prefrontal cortex was surgically removed in Pilgrim State Hospital. I would compare this section for its empathy to the lines in "Song of Myself" where Whitman compassionately cares for an escaping slave. As Whitman put it in "Song of Myself," "I do not ask the wounded person how he feels; I myself must become the wounded person." Whitman's tenderness, his nurturing of the frightened, fugitive, former slave is modulated and reassuring. Ginsberg is using Carl more as a warning and an indictment of a failed system:

> I'm with you in Rockland
>> where you bang on the catatonic piano the soul
>> is innocent and immortal it should never die
>> ungodly in an armed madhouse

Ginsberg's reiterated plea of "I'm with you in Rockland" acts almost as a soothing chant juxtaposed to the hyperbolic burlesque of Carl's acts, his confinement due to the murder of his twelve secretaries as he screams in his straightjacket that he is "losing the game of the actual ping pong of the abyss." Solomon spent six years in Pilgrim State in Meadowbrook, Long Island subjected to electric shock therapy or overdosed with insulin. In such circumstances, Ginsberg's tone cannot be quite as warm as Whitman's but his commitment is underlined by the refrain, repeated seventeen times, of "I'm with you in Rockland"—the name signifying both prison and the elimination of feeling for the sake of adjustment such institutions value. The section is an expression of a rare identification, and acceptance of personal responsibility, answering Cain's querulous question of "am I my brother's keeper?" with a litany of affirmation.

The ending lines for each of these first three sections provide magnificent moments of crescendo and resolution, what poet Gregory Corso once called "brilliant shock." The use of Christ's last supposed words on the cross—"eli eli lamma lamma sabacthani"—fused into an image of resurrection through the saxophone cry "of America's naked mind for love" offers a soaring conclusion to part one. The "mad generation" fleeing Moloch, carrying flowers down to the river at the end of part two sustains the velocity and tragic zaniness of the poem. Carl Solomon, at the end of part three, who in Ginsberg's dream arrives "dripping from a sea-journey on the highway across America in tears to the door of my cottage in the Western night" appears as a talismanic cipher of human suffering and magnanimity.

Ginsberg's poem, like T.S. Eliot's "The Waste Land," is almost 500 lines long, both less than half the size of Whitman's "Song of Myself." All three of these poems exist in an epic dimension, what Pound once defined in a letter to his mother as what occurs when the of a voice of a nation comes through the mouth of a poet. With a form like the epic, using history to explore the revealing values of a culture, the problem for the poet might be in creating an ending that fulfills the ambition of the poem.

Eliot, who wrote the early draft of his poem in a Swiss

sanitarium, while being treated with Benzedrine after a nervous breakdown, ended his extended and mournful complaint against the present with a Sanskrit word *"Shantih"*—or the peace that transcends understanding. The word is repeated three times with the effect of a dirge or a plaintive echo. Quite famously, and entirely without precedent in any poetic tradition, Eliot annotated his poem, providing fifty-four biblical, classical, or renaissance sources for some of his lines. In an essay called "Tradition and the Individual Talent," Eliot proposed that literature often worked this way, reinterpreting the past in a fresh context. This was exactly what Ginsberg was doing with Whitman's "Song of Myself" in "Howl."

A footnote, after all, is a scholarly communication, one quite without the lyric immediacy suitable for most poetry. These notes, Eliot maintained, were only meant for his readers, and he ignored them on the rare occasions when he read the poem in public. Ginsberg was reading *The Waste Land* while working on his poem and, in *Journals: Mid-Fifties*, quotes Eliot's compositional clue: "These fragments I have shored against my ruins." "Howl" ends with an extended singular "Footnote," though it is remarkably lyrical, unconventional, and vastly different from Eliot's more elliptical allusions to the sources of his inspiration.

Earlier in the poem, Ginsberg alludes to prayer, pilgrimage, and resurrection, and he begins the "Footnote" with a dithyrambic repetition of the word "Holy!" beaten, as if on a drum or a gong, fifteen times consecutively. It is a magnification, perhaps, of Whitman's claim that "I hear and behold God in every object" and his heretical notion –"Divine am I inside and out and I make holy whatever I touch or am touched from." Ginsberg uses the word "holy" over seventy times in the section, mostly followed by exclamation marks, in this case more an expression of awe than wonder. But it was what he included in his holy accounting that seemed so offensive to listeners like Hollander or the poet James Dickey, who compared the effect of the poem to the linguistic disorder of the Tower of Babel story in a piece in *The Sewanee Review*.

The Triumvirate

Dickey may have been thinking of the beginning lines of the "Footnote" which could have seemed so tasteless and meaningless to him. After the initial repetition of the word "Holy!" Ginsberg imagines:

> The world is holy! The soul is holy! The skin is holy!
> The nose is holy! The tongue and cock and
> hand and asshole holy!
> Everything is holy! everybody's holy! everywhere is
> holy! everyday is in eternity! Everyman's an
> angel!
> The bum's as holy as the seraphim! the madman as
> holy as you my soul are holy!

Of course the human rectum exits in an orifice which is a hole of sorts, but with no pun intended, the Hebrew root *kadosh*, "holy," means separate, suggesting a division between what is considered sacred and everything outside of the tabernacle that exists in a more profane sphere. Ginsberg's universal extension of holiness had to startle his audience—how can the bum be as holy as the child angels surrounding the throne of the Old Testament God, my grandmother might have anxiously queried? How can the groaning saxophone, the jazzbands, or the railroad locomotive exist on the same plane as the cock and the asshole? The formulation is anti-hierarchical and essentially religious. Ginsberg might have gotten this notion from listening to D.T. Suzuki's talks on Zen when he was an undergraduate at Columbia, from Kerouac, or from his own Buddhist inquiries, but he is also clearly attempting to refute the exponents of social conventions like Hollander, who would be so outraged by the poem.

This hypnotic concluding section is a chanting catharsis, an extended plea for compassion, sympathy, and inclusion, an ecstatic blessing, while at the same time asking for atonement for the transgressions of his generation. The entire footnote, which Ginsberg admitted developed from his memory of an extreme wail he once heard in a madhouse, especially with its concluding allusions to forgiveness, charity, and the "kindness of the soul," functions like a dervish dance, a rhapsody of grief and joy, a soaring transcendence of sorrow.

Sixty years after its composition, "Howl" stands as a juggernaut of modern poetry, a poem of enormous scope and relevance, an enduring, apocalyptic, American poem.

Ginsberg's Farm

JT: In what other ways did Burroughs influence you?

AG: With books: Kafka, Korzybski's *Science and Sanity*, Spengler's *Decline of the West,* which he gave to Kerouac, Blake, Rimbaud, Yeats' *A Vision*, Cocteau's *Opium.*

Interview with Ginsberg, *Partisan Review*

In early September of 1973, after an infernal nine-day heat wave in New York City, my wife Mellon and I set out for Cherry Valley. A few months earlier, I had sent Ginsberg essays that I had just published on the Beat Generation in two eminent journals, *The American Scholar* and *Partisan Review.* Ginsberg understood that the piece in *The American Scholar*, "The Beat Generation and the Continuing American Revolution" was probably the most positive recognition his group had received in the two decades since their original breakthrough publications. He invited me up to Cherry Valley to talk.

As in some proverbial fairy tale, the heavy downpour and ominous clouds that pursued us during the two hundred miles we drove suddenly changed to glorious sunshine when we approached the nestling hills that protect Cherry Valley. A village of eight hundred inhabitants, Cherry Valley is located in upstate

New York, about fifty miles west of Albany, near Cooperstown, the town named after the patrician family of James Fenimore Cooper. We passed our signpost, the poet Charles Plymell's house, situated just across from a triangularly shaped building, and weaved our way along four asphalt miles of left and right turns. Stopping at the Committee on Poetry mailbox, we relieved its contents as instructed, and perilously proceeded for another mile, jostling along a bumpy, pitted, dirt road.

My ride, in those heady days, was an Austin Mini, a small, square, British breadbox of a vehicle that quivered with every crease in the road. In those days, the Mini was used as a racer and only weighed twelve hundred pounds. I thought of it as a motorcycle with a thin jacket. I had purchased it new for twelve hundred dollars—a dollar a pound, the price of meat—because it was so easy to park in New York. Just before my marriage, picking up our wedding bands, the Mini had been rammed in its rear. In a giddy moment, I had foolishly pasted thirteen American flag decals into the reamed back end. I may have been anticipating the painter Jasper Johns, but the concave assemblage attracted the attention of too many policemen, some of whom demanded to know the significance of those bent flags twisting in every direction.

Outside of Ginsberg's farmhouse were two battered old cars and a rusty pickup. These vehicles seemed to suggest the Beat point of departure, the notion of being so downtrodden, defeated, and wrecked by the havoc of experience that one had nothing to lose by honest confession of the truth. We pulled up to the pandemonium of Ginsberg's three barking dogs and the bristling outrage of our own Irish setter, Shantih, who occupied the entire back seat of the Mini. Allen emerged to greet us, immediately intrigued by the diminutive Mini, as cars this small were rarely seen then in the U.S.

Ginsberg, with what seemed like a quizzical glance, asked whether we had ever met before. In fact we had, in a bar called Stanley's on Avenue B near Tompkins Square Park, but then I was just a face in a crowd. If I detected a trace of suspicion in Ginsberg's query, I was already used to that from interviews I had attempted with his friends, William Burroughs, Lucian Carr, and Herbert Huncke, who sized me up initially as an undercover F.B.I. man or informant. The Beats had been systematically disparaged by academicians and I made my living in a university.

Ginsberg's old farmhouse was situated on seventy acres of gently rolling land that had lain fallow for many years. The farm had few amenities: no electricity, no insulation, no heat other than a wood/coal Kalamazoo kitchen stove, and a broken, outside, hand-powered water pump. The inside walls were knotty pine boards and the furniture was quite worn and weathered—most of it had been in the house when Ginsberg purchased it.

We entered through the kitchen—illuminated by gas lamps emitting the softest light—to meet Ginsberg's life companion, Peter Orlovsky, who was furiously slicing beets, forearms and fingers raddled like Diggory Venn's in Thomas Hardy's novel. Peter showed us up a flight of stairs to our room with a wooden bed on the floor that he had constructed for our visit. Peter was good with tools and with his hands. A gruff, outspoken, moody man, I felt an immediate connection when he told me that as a young man he had worked as a field laborer on some of the last farmland in Queens, just adjacent to the campus where I teach.

That entire week, Peter roared around the farm in his tractor as he vigorously worked the land, mended fences, cut and stacked cords of wood, canned tomatoes, and pickled beets. Peter's presence seemed larger than his body. Direct and rugged, a dynamo of activity, his gravel voice rose from the pit of his stomach with conviction and command. The most energetic of men—I never saw him rest—his movements were stylized and graceful, leaps in the dance of his work.

Despite the oncoming fall chill, he was usually bare-chested, and he reminded my wife of Mellors in *Lady Chatterley's Lover.* I wondered whether he was taking speed, since I knew one of the reasons Ginsberg had purchased the farm was Peter's reliance on Methedrine, which he would score in the East Village. During the 1960s, Ginsberg was constantly giving readings through the United States and Europe, and when he was away Peter could be tempted. So the farm existed as an opportunity for health and recovery.

Peter had prepared a lunch of noodles flavored with basil and tomatoes from the garden. At the table, I met Carl Solomon who was staying at the farm that week. Carl was the dedicatee of "Howl" and part three of the poem presented him as a figure of mythic suffering and absurdity. He had first met Ginsberg when they were fellow inmates at the Columbia Psychiatric Institute in 1947. It had been Carl Solomon, working as an editor in 1952, who had accepted William Burroughs' first novel, *Junky*. Subsequently, Solomon spent years at Pilgrim State Psychiatric Hospital in Meadowbrook, New York where he received many shock treatments. Now he was medicated with Thorazine, living with his mother in the Bronx, and working in a bookstore.

An autodidactic intellectual of the old order, Solomon was gifted with the kind of curiosity that had led him to discover writers like Artaud, Genet, and other European avant-gardes long before they became known in America. Now, however, he confessed that literary experiment no longer interested him as much. Recently, he told me, he had reread *War and Peace* and was now going through Proust again. He also claimed that he no longer took any political position, and furthermore, that he accepted the possibility that he had no recognizable identity. His doctors had taught him to abandon all philosophical questioning and live from day to day. This avatar of the age of anxiety seemed to have an overwhelming need for orderly existence. He lived in what he termed the "absolute straight present" with no distractions provoked by drugs or alcohol. Though the anarchic rage of one of the men who had inspired "Howl" had been chastened by experience and dissipated, his essential sweetness and gentility was still evident.

After lunch, Carl, who had published two short, pithy books of reflections with City Lights, showed me several sketches he was working on, including a hilarious parody of a James Bond sex fantasy. Even in its apparently unrevised state, the work had some eloquence, and I recommended that he send the Bond parody to *Playboy* or *The New Yorker*, though I sensed that he lacked the confidence to do it.

The Triumvirate

I had many questions for Ginsberg, who was sitting outside with Richard Clark, the master of a Zen Center in nearby Sharon Springs. Ginsberg was preparing to leave for three months of meditation and study with a Tibetan Lama, Rinpoche Chogyam Trumpa Tulka in Jackson Hole, Wyoming, and I saw Ginsberg needed time alone with Clark.

Mellon and I took Shantih through a meadow to a pond, and we found a little shack that Ginsberg later told me was inhabited by a hermit. When we rejoined Ginsberg and Clark, I asked Ginsberg about Jack Kerouac. He emphasized the enormous pain Kerouac felt because of the five-year difficulty in getting *On the Road* published. The ultimate betrayal, Kerouac felt, was the book's reception when it was finally released. Kerouac, Ginsberg maintained, had fully expected to be welcomed as an American novelist, not condemned as an inspiration of delinquency. Kerouac never felt as alienated as Ginsberg or Burroughs, but embraced his country with Whitman's egalitarian perspective. When critics associated him with deviance and the chaos of degenerative change, he lapsed into Melvillean despair.

Dinner was a communal affair, the fruit of the tomatoes and string beans I had helped Ginsberg harvest that afternoon. I had written a dissertation on Henry James and found it somewhat unorthodox to be inquiring about the origins of Ginsberg's literary group while bending and stooping to pick vegetables in the soil. I had a little notebook in my back pocket in which I would scribble with dirty fingers while Allen resolved matters of Beat history or Burroughs' and Kerouac's fiction. He seemed as eager to talk about their work as his own. I felt more like an anthropologist than a biographer. Instead of the cloistered sanctuary of the library archive, I could smell the earth and hear the birds sing as I learned.

In the evening, as I helped Carl shuck the corn and wash the beans, Ginsberg sang a rendition of some Blake poems, while accompanying himself on a hand organ. The kitchen was the communal center of the farm. Redolent with herbs and spices and the vegetables Peter was canning, it was a place of warmth and companionship. Allen himself was the mother hen, concerned about everyone's needs. He baked us an apple pie with apples gathered on the farm and the delicious winey odor permeated the house.

Peter's brother, Julius, set the table. He was a catatonic schizophrenic in Peter's care who could go for days without sleeping or eating and rarely spoke. I wondered whether Julius, who sat by himself in a corner without sharing any of the food, represented the spiritual lesson of the Beat phenomenon. Under ordinary circumstances, he could have been sentenced to a life in some mental institution. Instead, with love and guidance, he had been taught to care for himself by those who cared most for him.

Later that evening, Julius, whose catatonia had been the subject of a film by Robert Frank, read me a passage from Timothy Leary's *Jail Notes*, and then discussed it with stolid conviction. His ability seemed like a testimonial, a rejoinder to our mutual need to only rely on institutional solutions for social problems. I thought the radical British psychiatrist R.D. Laing would have enjoyed meeting Julius Orlovsky.

That night, Ginsberg asked to read a chapter of my manuscript, in progress, on the Beats. I gave him the chapter on Burroughs, and the next morning he wanted to talk about it. Mellon suggested turning on the small tape machine I used for interviewing, and we spoke for two hours. Carl Solomon participated, while Peter fed us porridge and tea, and then resumed canning beets and tomatoes. When contemplating the fiction and theories of William Burroughs, some sustenance is useful. The result was the interview on Burroughs' work that would appear in *Partisan Review*. I still believe it exists as the most coherent approach to Burroughs' work.

The Kerouac Conundrum: A Reputation Study

"Fame is like old newspapers
Blowing down Bleecker Street"
    Kerouac, quoted by Alene Lee

"Fame is no more than the sum of all the misunderstandings that gather around a new name."
    Rilke on Rodin

I would say Kerouac offered his heart to the United States and the United States rejected his heart. He realized what suffering the United States was in for, and so the tragedy of America.... America, by his day, was sick. Militarily sick. Military-Industrial complex had taken over. Hard-heartedness had taken over. Everything that as a Canuck peasant Kerouac hated had taken over: the mechanization, the impersonality, the homogenization, the money-grabbing, the disrespect for person. And vast wars—the attack on the provincial in the wars. So I would say America broke his heart.
    Allen Ginsberg in *Jack Kerouac's Road* (1987).

Beat Transnationalism

In the past fifty years, there has probably been more biographical interest in Jack Kerouac than in any other modern American novelist. On my bookshelf, I have a very intriguing oral biography by Barry Gifford and Lawrence Lee—although I know that the recollections of friends and rivals can often be compromised by the fog of memory, the vanity of jealousy, or any one of a number of other subjective factors. The danger of this genre is that the anecdotal is often just above the level of gossip and frequently romantic gloss, malicious or misinformed.

Sitting on the bookshelf are a half dozen memoirs by former wives or lovers, some written with cudgels and sharpened axes like Joan Haverty's *Nobody's Wife*. There are also another half-dozen biographies, mostly flawed attempts, limited either by estate prohibitions or inadequate access, haphazard writing skills, faulty judgment, an undeveloped sense of literary history, or the inability to distinguish the actual from literary legend or self-perpetuated myth.

Ann Charters, who wrote the first of these, at least had the advantage of knowing Kerouac and compiling a bibliography with him, but the Kerouac Estate denied her permission to quote from his letters or notebooks, vitiating the result. Gerald Nicosia's *Memory Babe* was published in 1983, a behemoth book of the sort that Henry James would have characterized as a loose and baggy monster whose relentless parade of facts would scatter, like a confusion of ants streaming in a dozen different directions. Nicosia, as Morris Dickstein pointed out in *The New York Times,* lacked the critical facility to measure the dynamic elements in Kerouac's fiction. Nicosia was followed by a sluggish stream of similarly routine and undistinguished attempts. In 1998, Ellis Amburn, who had been Kerouac's last editor and might have known better, offered a travesty of rumor and misinterpretation in *Subterranean Kerouac.*

Most biographers are only capable of wooden prose. It is rare to find any like Richard Ellmann or Leon Edel, who write with style and imagination. There were a couple of brighter and briefer biographical inquiries into aspects of Kerouac's life along the way, an insightful take by poet Tom Clark and Victor-Levy Beaulieu who explored Kerouac's French-Canadian roots in *A Chicken Essay*, and most recently by Joyce Johnson who had known Kerouac intimately.

Her book, *The Voice Is All,* is written with a poised balance between narrative and literary analysis, with the most nuanced view so far of Kerouac's volatile moodiness and considerable complexities. Fusing a lot of intuition with personal observation, Johnson is able to identify Kerouac's emotional dynamics with more sympathy than any of her predecessors:

> By nature, he was silent, and when he was sober, he probably kept most of his angry, unacceptable ideas to himself. When he was drunk enough, he would express them with the alcohol-ignited vehemence of someone dangerously certain that he alone sees the truth.

Kerouac knew he was a writer from the age of eleven, and the Berg Collection of the New York Public Library has reams of his early stuff, like the newspaper accounts of imagined horse races and baseball games. A young man of working-class origins from the somewhat provincial factory town of Lowell, Massachusetts, Kerouac had been a fullback on the high school team, and his speed and agility won him an athletic scholarship to Columbia University, where he would meet Ginsberg and Burroughs.

After dropping out of Columbia early in World War Two, he signed on for six bomb runs with the Merchant Marine, transporting explosives to the European theater. He lived with his parents in a very small apartment in Queens. They had relocated to a poor section called Ozone Park, although the only park space in the area was devoted to huge cemeteries

He agreed to go on a seventh bomb run but never departed— the ship was hit by a torpedo with no survivors. His father had been diagnosed with cancer of the spleen and Kerouac decided to care for him while his mother continued to work in a shoe factory. In the cramped kitchen in Ozone Park, he worked on a traditional fiction, about his Lowell years, that he called *The Town and the City*. The novel was very much an apprenticeship effort, with imitations of Hemingway and Fitzgerald, and influenced by the overwritten, rhetorical lushness of Thomas Wolfe. He was taking a class at The New School taught by Alfred Kazin, and he showed him what he was writing. Kazin, a leading critic of American literature, recommended that Roger Giroux, a prescient editor then working at Harcourt Brace, read the manuscript. Giroux accepted it, but forced Kerouac to eliminate a quarter of his manuscript. The process of revision, catering to Giroux's demands, was painful for Kerouac. The novel appeared in 1950; like most first novels, it sold poorly and received little notice.

For a year, Kerouac struggled to discover a less conventional means for his fiction. In the spring of 1951, he came down with a serious case of phlebitis, the potentially fatal formation of a blood clot in his leg. With his leg in traction in a V.A. hospital in Queens, he received a long, sprawling letter from a friend named Neal Cassady, written with a raw power practically as one exfoliating sentence, uninhibited by grammatical proprieties. He had met Cassady a few years earlier—Neal was naked when he answered his door on their first meeting in 1947, stunning Kerouac enough to know he wanted to make Cassady the subject of a novel.

Using Neal's letter as a stylistic template, in April of 1951, Kerouac wrote his first version of the story of Neal Cassady, which he would call *On the Road*. Typing very rapidly, working for up to twenty hours a day, the novel was written on a scroll of pages, which Kerouac had taped together, so he would not have to slow down to insert a new page into his typewriter. When it was completed, virtually in the rush of one long, haphazardly punctuated sentence, Kerouac had used the real names of his friends who were its characters, which would have made any publisher susceptible to libel suits. He understood that, with his novel, he had created something new, as well as an epic announcement about the changes occurring in American life in

The Triumvirate

the post-war period.

In the flush of his enthusiasm, Kerouac displayed his one hundred and twenty foot scroll on his editor's desk. Surprised by the unconventional presentation, Robert Giroux immediately raised the issue of revision. Feeling rejected, always uncomfortable with authority, Kerouac stalked out of the office, saying that his story had been dictated to him by the Holy Ghost. The implication, of course, was that revision would be blasphemous, but Kerouac's abrupt departure was also a radical revocation of the symbiotic relationship between writers and their editors. He was spurning the sacred cow of the literary experience. It cost him his relationship with Giroux, then probably the most important fiction editor on the American publishing scene. It was the beginning of his problematic publication history.

Kerouac knew that with *On the Road* he had reached a pinnacle of "peak maturity," that in 1951 he had been "blowing such mad poetry and literature that [he'd] look back years later with amazement and chagrin that [he couldn't] do it anymore." During the six years that Kerouac had to wait for *On the Road* to appear, he wrote another dozen books while living with his mother in Queens, but sometimes on pennies a day in skid row San Francisco or in a rooftop stone hovel in Mexico City. These seemingly unpublishable books were evidence of a writer's stubborn faith in his own capacities, or the sign that he was helpless to stop, caught in the compulsion to record his feelings even if only for a singular audience composed of himself and a few friends, like Allen Ginsberg.

In 1955, the critic and Lost Generation writer, Malcolm Cowley, intervened and persuaded Viking to reconsider the novel. In his Reader's Report to Viking, Cowley called On *the Road* "the voice of a new generation. "The observation was both cogent and astute. Kerouac's reluctance to revise and conform the unprecedented rush of the scroll version with commas, more conventionally punctuated sentences, and chapters, delayed the project. When Kerouac understood that unless *On the Road* was published, he had little chance of any future success, he allowed Helen Taylor and Keith Jennison, the Viking editors, to conventionalize the manuscript. After *On the Road* became a best seller, a number of the books he had written from 1951 to 1957 began to appear; others, like his masterpiece, *Visions of Cody,* would only appear posthumously.

The key factor in catapulting Kerouac's reputation was Gilbert Milstein's review in *The New York Times* on September 5, 1957. By calling the novel an "authentic work of art," whose publication was an "historic occasion," Milstein was making a very large claim. He found sections of the novel "in which the writing is of a beauty almost breathtaking" and some writing on jazz "that has never been equaled in American fiction, either for its insight, style, or technical virtuosity." *On the Road* was a major novel, he claimed, and like Hemingway's *The Sun Also Rises*, was a sign of a new sensibility—"the most beautifully executed, the clearest and the most important utterance yet made by the generation Kerouac himself named years ago as 'beat,' and whose principal avatar he is."

It must be admitted that Milstein's rave review had been something of a fluke. While the daily issue of the newspaper had a much broader reach than the Sunday book section, Milstein was not the regular reviewer. Charles Poore, who had respectfully greeted *The Town and the City* and Orville Prescott, the regulars, were both on summer holiday when the galleys of *On the Road* appeared in early August. They might easily have deigned to review the book or disparaged its excess, its fusion of desperation and joy. As the third-string music critic, a jazz aficionado, Milstein was in another department, but he responded enthusiastically to the jazz descriptions in the novel.

Milstein's praise put the novel on the best-seller list for a few weeks. There was a quick second printing and the Book Find Club featured it. Kerouac's life changed drastically. Overnight, he had become famous, although fame can make any unknown artist into an immediate target. It was possible, Milstein had conceded, that some of the novel's reception might be condescending and the initial sign of this was David Dempsey's review in the Sunday *New York Times Book Review,* a much more cautious appraisal.

"In Pursuit of 'Kicks,'" the title the editors of the *Book Review* gave to Dempsey's piece, was a cultural sign of disapproval. With a somewhat Victorian perspective, Dempsey suggested that the sideshow of "freaks" on display in Kerouac's novel "flirted with depravity" and introduced the reader to an "assortment of migratory decadents" who Kerouac was unwilling or unable to morally evaluate. While the novel was entertaining and descriptive, Kerouac failed to delineate any character development. His central character, Dean, was pathological and the journeys pointless.

A week later, *Time*, with the largest magazine circulation in America, accused Kerouac of justifying "the fevered young who twitch around the nation's jukeboxes and brawl pointlessly in the midnight streets." In the view of the establishment, then, Kerouac was abetting delinquency and social breakdown, and the label would stick like chewing gum on the underside of a shoe.

Most of the other reviews were similarly condemnatory. The eminent Carlos Baker, Hemingway's pal and biographer, was left "sad and blank" by what he found to be "a dizzy travelogue." The reviewer in the *Chicago Tribune* thought the novel was "completely uncontrolled" and that Kerouac "slobbers words." Another critic in *The Atlantic* found the novel monotonous and repetitious. It was "verbal goofballs'" for the Saturday *Review*, it seemed "infantile, perversely negative" to the reviewer in the *Herald Tribune*, and it lacked seriousness according to the critic in *Commonweal*. The novel was compared to "a slob running a temperature" in the *Hudson Review*, and in *Encounter* the reviewer was dismayed by a "series of Neanderthal grunts." In *The San Francisco Chronicle*, Kenneth Rexroth described the novel as the work of a "furious square" filled with characters with the intelligence of "May flies and little children." The Beat craze, Rexroth predicted, would soon be as "dead as Davy Crockett's caps." The meanest review was written for *The Nation*, by Herbert Gold, a novelist no one now remembers, who had been one of Kerouac's classmates at

Columbia. Gold decided the novel had been composed for a group of "unleashed zazous" (whatever that could mean) and deplored Kerouac's linguistic flights, and the freedom of his characters to express their exuberance as naturally as "Whoee." Kerouac, Gold concluded, was frantic, and his delinquent characters suffered from protracted adolescence.

By far the most damning indictment of Kerouac as a writer would be an essay by the social commentator, Norman Podhoretz, another one of Kerouac's former classmates at Columbia. Podhoretz was determined to prove that Kerouac just could not write and his essay, "The Know-Nothing Bohemians" would appear in the extremely influential *Partisan Review*, in the spring of 1958. The piece, rabid almost in its vehemence, was as much an attack on Kerouac's circle as on Kerouac himself. Podhoretz decided the Beats stood for a know-nothing, populist sentiment that was only "hostile to civilization,"—they worshipped "primitivism, instinct, energy, 'blood.'" This was terminology that had been used to describe Adolph Hitler's circle of followers in the 1930s.

According to Podhoretz, the vitality that Kerouac drew from jazz was merely a means of "expressing contempt for coherent, rational discourse." Kerouac was the exponent of a bitter anti-intellectualism, deriving from emotion and inciting violence. Podhoretz' heavy-handed judgment is reminiscent of the unsung critic in *Le Figaro* in Paris reviewing *Madame Bovary* who concluded Gustave Flaubert was not a writer— "M. Flaubert n'est pas un ecrivain." In Podhoretz' reading, Kerouac's bohemian intention was to "kill the intellectuals who can talk coherently, kill the people who can sit still for five minutes at a time, kill those incomprehensible characters who are capable of getting seriously involved with a woman, a job, a cause."

As a novelist, Podhoretz declared that in *On the Road* "nothing that happens has any dramatic reason for happening" and Kerouac lacks the ability to articulate his thoughts and feeling and in fact demonstrates "his simple inability to express anything in words." This stands as the roughest treatment

The Triumvirate

any American writer has received since Edgar Allen Poe was mauled by the minister, Rufus Griswold, who insinuated that Poe's character was so flawed he had illicit relations with his illiterate aunt and mother-in-law.

Like Griswold, Podhoretz' point of departure was his own rigid morality. It is no accident that with Irving Kristol he did much to solidify the nascent neo-conservative movement behind Ronald Reagan. As one of Kerouac's later admirers, the journalist Seymour Krim so pithily put it, to the critics of *On the Road*, like Podhoretz or his teacher, the literary critic Lionel Trilling, Kerouac's world may have resembled "a psychotic picnic spiked with bombersized dexies." Kerouac was "regarded very fishily as a simple-minded athletic type run amok," and his reputation would be "charred and uncertain." *On the Road*, Krim argued, was part of a revolt against the intimidating force of a cerebral formalism and T.S. Eliot's anti-romantic notions of "escape from personality" that dominated American academies in the 1950s. The birth of a new style emerges from a radical change in values, Krim argued, which Kerouac's detractors were unable to see.

Podhoretz, at the beginning of his piece, made a point of commenting on Kerouac's "photogenic countenance (unshaven, of course, and an unruly crop of rich black hair falling over his forehead)." And the comment seems less a literary criticism than the sign of incipient jealousy. The best illustration of this tension, and the notion of Kerouac as a facile phenomenon, may stem from Truman Capote's maliciously dismissive quip that *On the Road* wasn't writing but merely typewriting. Capote's *Breakfast at Tiffany's* was coming out and he may have resented the attention that Kerouac was receiving. Capote's frivolous remark, of course, is belied by the fact that half of Kerouac's novels were initially written in pencil in spiral notebooks.

While it seems awkward to reduce Podhoretz' or Capote's objections to Kerouac to the issue of personality, the problem may have something to do with Ann Charters' observation that so many of Kerouac's readers "came away with the indelible impression that he personified the lifestyle he described."

Cowley commented that he looked like the movie star, Gregory Peck. My own choice for comparison would be the look of bruised vulnerability in an actor like Montgomery Clift. For the critic James Wolcott, Kerouac's look of "tough wounded masculinity" was reminiscent of Marlon Brando, to whom Kerouac once wrote about acquiring film rights to *On the Road*.

Writing can often compensate for irresolvable personal difficulties, and Kerouac was tormented by unresolved relationships. He was conflicted by his own contradictions: essentially shy, he became an extroverted entertainer when drunk. He was, by turns, exuberant and full of despair. In the flesh, as Seymour Krim has so bluntly observed, he could be "infantile, insecure, paranoid, desperate." Instead of the intrepid traveler he depicts in *On the Road*, he was afraid of driving or hitchhiking, afraid of falling under the wheels of a train, terrified of flying. Most of his travel was with homemade sandwiches on a Greyhound bus, and most of his life he lived with his mother.

Neither Podhoretz nor Capote knew Kerouac well enough to know any of this—to them he was just a handsome hunk getting all the attention which Podhoretz may have felt was undeserved and Capote certainly wanted for himself. However, jealous or not, they caused indelible damage.

I would like to offer a personal illustration. A few years ago, a professorial poet-pal asked me to hear a piano player who was becoming his accompanist in a cramped bar below ground level on Houston Street, in New York City. The jazz-inflected poetry my friend writes and performs is the result of a fusion form advanced by Kerouac when he was an unknown in Greenwich Village clubs like the Figaro and the Village Vanguard in the 1950s. As we were leaving, I told him I was working on a piece on Kerouac in Mexico, circa 1950-55. His response was cutting: As a writer, my friend grumbled, "Kerouac was only suitable for adolescents." I wonder whether he would offer the same evaluation of Mark Twain after reading *Adventures of Huckleberry Finn,* or even of Hemingway because of the Nick

The Triumvirate

Adams stories.

It is true that after the publication of *On the Road,* there was a sudden change in Kerouac's literary visibility after years of anonymity. Translations of *On the Road* were commissioned in Germany, France, and Italy. James Laughlin, at New Directions, agreed to print an abridged version of Kerouac's most experimental, Proustian book, *Visions of Cody.* Barney Rosset, at Grove Press, in New York, decided to publish two novels Kerouac had written in 1953, The *Subterraneans* and *Doctor Sax.*

Kerouac claimed he had written *The Subterraneans* in three days. The short novel about a love affair of Kerouac's with an African-American woman crossed a controversial barrier in American fiction at a time when thirty states still enforced anti-miscegenation laws. Kerouac's love story went further in the actual measurement of sexual feeling than D.H. Lawrence or Miller had. Consider, for example, his description of female orgasm near the end of his novel:

> Finally I had her, I pray for it to come, I can hear her breathing harder, I hope against hope it's time, a noise in the hall (or whoop of drunkards next door) takes her mind off and she can't make it and laughs—but when she does make it I hear her crying, whimpering, the shuddering electrical female orgasm makes her sound like a little girl crying, moaning in the night, it lasts a good twenty seconds and when it's over she moans, 'O, why can't it last longer, and 'O when will I when you do?'

The novel was published with a key introduction by Henry Miller, who generously praised Kerouac's ability to record what he heard, a true American sound:

> alive to the idiomatic lingo of his time—the swing, the beat, the disjunctive metaphoric

rhythm which comes so fast, so wild, so scrimmaged, so unbelievably albeit delectably mad that when transmitted to paper no one recognizes it. None but the poets, that is.

Other notices were much less generous. A reviewer in *The New Republic* was persuaded of "no sign that the author or his characters know what they are talking about." In *The New York Times*, David Dempsey (again!) with a cruel barb, maintained that Kerouac's story "seeps out like sludge from a leaky drain pipe." *Time* pursued that image by nominating Kerouac for the awful distinction of "latrine laureate." And *Newsweek* concluded the novel was "tasteless"

Suddenly, Kerouac was able to sell stories and sketches to places like *Esquire, Playboy,* and *Holiday*. Viking asked for a sequel to *On the Road* and Kerouac began *The Dharma Bums*. There were several Hollywood overtures and negotiations for the film rights to *On the Road*. They collapsed but *The Subterraneans* was optioned and adapted, although afflicted by a coarse sensationalism. .

Kerouac was interviewed by *The Saturday Review, The New York Herald Tribune*, and John Wingate's television program *Nightbeat*, where he notoriously declared that he was "waiting for God to show me his face." He cut a record with the entertainer Steve Allen, who would later invite him on his television program to read from *On the Road*, and he started reading his poems in Village clubs, like the Vanguard, accompanied by jazz musicians. This fusion of jazz and poetry was a new mode that would find many adherents and imitators.

This imitation was also problematic. In San Francisco, after the successful Russian Sputnik space launching, the gossip columnist Herb Caen invented the snickering term "Beatnik" to apply to Kerouac's followers. A reporter in the *San Francisco Examiner* characterized them as pathetic, self-pitying, and degenerate. Popular media associated the Beats with crime and perversion. *Life Magazine* presented a picture essay that parodied the Beats as so lost in a haze of marijuana smoke that

The Triumvirate

their children were left unattended on the kitchen floor playing with beer cans.

When *The Dharma Bums* was published, in the fall of 1958, Ginsberg wrote a heartfelt tribute in *The Village Voice*. Most of the other reviews were extremely negative. In *The New York Times,* Charles Poore found it a juvenile parody. J. Donald Adams, in his influential column in the *Times Book Review*, deplored what he saw as a world of "drugs, drunkenness, and aimless wandering." William Bittner, in *The Saturday Review,* complained about a "muddle of maturity with adolescent blubbering."

The Saturday Review can certainly be considered a voice of the establishment, and in an essay called "Epitaph for the Dead Beats," the polished poet, John Ciardi, dismissed Kerouac as a rebel adolescent suffering from a narcissistic illness, which Ciardi found dull. His fiction, Ciardi decided, was "unreadable." Ciardi's attack was followed by another one by Robert Brustein, "The Cult of Unthink," in *Horizon,* and John Updike's clever parody of Kerouac's style in *The New Yorker.*

As the critic, James Wolcott, has observed, Kerouac may have been the last American writer without either cynicism or protective guile. "He seemed to regard tabloid ink as if it were his own spilled blood," Wolcott perceptively noted, and Kerouac's reaction to the bad reviews led to a gradual withdrawal from the literary community. Although he wrote to the end, he retreated into what he called "the joyous disease" of alcoholism for the remaining decade of his life.

Kerouac died in St. Petersburg, Florida in 1969. Writing had become difficult for him, and he was fully aware of the diminution of his own powers. His last novel, *Vanity of Duluoz*, had been trashed universally. Before he died, he was completing a short novel about a runaway African-American kid he named Pic, a clue to the picaresque tradition he had always pursued. He sat in the bleachers of the minor league baseball team in St. Petersburg, then still restricted to African-Americans, because he was still listening, trying to capture the language he needed to give Pic.

His novelist friend, John Clellon Holmes, in an essay called "The Great Rememberer," addressed the dismaying critical reputation Kerouac had at the end of his life:

> Though he has already created a larger body of work than any of his contemporaries, to most people his name summons up a carefree do-nothing sensation-hunter. Though that body of work creates a dense, personal world that is as richly detailed as any such American literary world since Faulkner, he is continually thought to be the poet of the pads and the bard of bebop. And though he is a prose innovator in the tradition of Joyce, whose stylistic experiments will bear comparison with any but the most radical avant-gardists of the century, he is constantly ticketed as some slangy, hitchhiking Jack London, bringing a whiff of marijuana and truck exhaust into the lending libraries. In short, the kind of writer that only America could produce, and that only America could so willfully misunderstand.

Fifteen years earlier, in a letter he sent to Stella Sampas, who would become this third wife, Kerouac predicted, "I am going to be famous, and the greatest writer of my generation, like Dostoevsky, and someday they'll see this . . ." Soon, after his death, that reputation began to change, and what seemed like a vain prediction was coming true.

Seymour Krim commented that Kerouac's primary value may be inspirational, and that observation has been echoed by artists like Bob Dylan, Ken Kesey, Thomas Pynchon, Leonard Cohen, Jim Morrison, Jim and Van Morrison, and Hunter S. Thompson. In the early 1970s, Joyce Johnson, working as an editor at McGraw-Hill, arranged for the publication of *Visions of Cody*. Other publishers then reprinted a series of Kerouac novels that were long out of print, had never appeared, or were

The Triumvirate

previously available only in paperback editions. This probably intensified the revival of interest in Kerouac, although young people had been so drawn to *On the Road* that they were using it as a springboard to travel in the United States.

Ginsberg was elected to the American Academy of the Arts in 1973, and Burroughs' election followed in 1981(after six years of nominations). In 1980, Governor George Dukakis of Massachusetts commissioned an astonishing monument to be constructed to commemorate Kerouac in his hometown of Lowell. Its eight ten foot high granite tablets, each engraved with a citation from another of his novels, dominate the town like a Stonehenge. The monument was unveiled in 1988, and there is probably no monument to a literary figure on the planet as central or imposing.

In 1982, the University of Colorado sponsored a weeklong celebration of the twenty-fifth anniversary of the publication of *On the Road.* In 1984, *Vanity Fair* asked me to do a piece on the Beats, a sign that the Beats had become mainstream rather than marginal. That sign was confirmed, perhaps, in 1990, when Rhino Records in Los Angeles released a four CD collection of Kerouac's spoken word poetry. By then, the bookstores in New York City were placing Kerouac's novels behind the cash registers so they could not be stolen.

In 1995, Viking Press published the first of two volumes of Kerouac's letters. Writing in the *New York Times,* Ann Douglas, the Parr Professor of literature at Columbia University, announced that Kerouac's work was "the most extensive experiment in language and literary form undertaken by an American writer of his generation."

That year, at the Whitney Museum show devoted to the painting and photography of the Beats, the scroll version of *On the Road* was displayed in a glass case. It had been purchased at auction at Christie's by James Irsay, the owner of the Indianapolis Colts football team, for 2.4 million dollars, the highest price paid at that point for any American literary manuscript. Now the scroll travels from museum to museum, and the scroll version has even been published by Viking Press exactly as Kerouac originally conceived it.

William Burroughs, commenting on Kerouac's popular appeal, wrote that Kerouac's books "sold a trillion Levi's, a million espresso coffee machines, and also sent countless kids on the road." He compared Kerouac to F. Scott Fitzgerald, as a generational spokesman whose effect "is immediate, as if a generation was waiting to be written."

In 1997, Kerouac's notebooks began to appear in *The Atlantic* and *The New Yorker*. A book of philosophical meditations Kerouac had written in Queens in the 1950s on the nature of Buddhism called *Some of the Dharma* was published by Viking, and there would be a stream of posthumously published fiction and poetry to follow. The nature writer, Verlyn Klinkenborg, would praise the publication of Kerouac's *The Book of Haiku* on the editorial page of *The New York Times*. The Library of America would publish two thick collections of Kerouac's fiction. Finally, for three months in the winter of 2007, the New York Public Library exhibited at its main branch, at 42nd Street and Fifth Avenue, the giant archival repository that had been acquired by its Berg Collection. It was surely a sign that Kerouac had come home.

Transnational Beat

> Can it be that we are all exiles? Is it possible that all of us are wandering strange lands?
>   Roberto Bolaño

> All men are lonely. But sometimes it seems to me that we Americans are the loneliest of all. Our hunger for foreign places and new ways has been almost like a national disease. Our literature is stamped with a quality of longing and unrest, and our writers have been great wanderers.
>   Carson McCullers, "Look Homeward Americans"

I. The Nomads

When the poet H.D.'s father, Dr. Charles Leander Doolittle, the stuffed shirt, distinguished Professor of Astronomy at the University of Pennsylvania, dismissed Ezra Pound's courtship of his daughter, Hilda, with the dismissive comment that "he's only a nomad," he meant that the flamboyant young suitor would never be able to properly provide for her. At the same time, though, was he not establishing what we now might see as a locus point for the emerging transnational character of some modern writers?

Pound would spend the next decade in London writing art and music criticism for *The New Age* and formulating the new principles for the Imagist poem. Dismayed by the disaster of World War I, he moved to Paris for five years, and then spent another twenty in Rapallo, forging *The Cantos* and getting embroiled in an overheated political cauldron. That folly led to twelve years of incarceration in a mental prison in Washington, D.C., ending with a final decade of haunted silence in Venice. It was certainly an unsettled path into new territory. Pound's motto was "Make It New," and like *Finnegan's Wake, The Cantos* required familiarity with half a dozen languages so it was, in character, a different and more demanding sort of literary medium.

When it works, language can express beauty and wonder but sometimes it acts as a border guard, a wall for insularity or elitism. It forms a central element in personal identity and a demarcation of cultural difference in any case. Pound, of course, had precursors in his blurring of national boundaries. Henry James expatriated to London after the Civil War, but absorbed himself in England as fully as T.S. Eliot after him, both such perfectly assimilated British gentlemen that some English literary historians conscript them as national possessions.

The prototypical transnational writer is Joseph Conrad, who wrote in English, which happened to be his fourth language. Born in Poland, his second language was an uneducated Russian, heard in one of the Czar's prisons where both his parents developed tuberculosis and died young. He learned French as a seaman in the French merchant marine. Retired from a career as a British seaman where he advanced from cabin boy to captain, he struggled to write. With his East European accent, he was forever insecure about his command of the English language, which was not the result of schooling but acquired pragmatically by work at sea. He had adventures to relate, stories of enigmatic spies, anarchists, and smugglers, the result of voyages around the world, and despite encouragement from writers like Ford Madox Ford and Henry James, finding the right words and the proper diction was a protracted torture for Conrad.

The Triumvirate

Writers often voyage to discover a new story in the manner of Melville in the Marquesan Islands, or to make one happen as Byron did in Greece, with drastic consequences. Modern writers, starting with Mark Twain or Jack London, may have left familiar shores because they have had more mobility and means. The issue becomes to what degree is the writer reporting—the novel as travelogue—or being affected by his new circumstances? Consider the difference between James Joyce, the Irishman living in Trieste and teaching at Berlitz language school, whose exclusive subject remained his hometown Dublin, and another Irishman, Samuel Beckett, living in Paris and writing in French. Some writers may absorb or react to their new surroundings more than others, like Elizabeth Bishop in Brazil or Roberto Bolaño who migrated through South America to Europe. All these writers seem, as Poe once put it, "wanderers of no fixed abode," or explorers of consciousness and conditioning, as an anthropologist might see it.

II. Interzone

For the Beats, Mexico was only a jumping off point, a logical first step because of its proximity and affordability. Burroughs had led the way to Mexico and beyond. His quest for yagé in South America in 1953 resulted in a remarkable collection of letters to Ginsberg, later published as *The Yagé Letters*. Drawn by Paul Bowles' emotionally resonant and ultimately shattering novel, *The Sheltering Sky,* Burroughs went to Tangiers, where he would spend most of the years from 1954-57. Writing under the influence of serious addictive substances, he worked on a sprawling, disorganized manuscript that would subsequently form the basis of *Naked Lunch* and the three novels that followed it.

Tangier was an international zone located in a French colony but governed haphazardly by French, Spanish, British, and Italian administrators, each of whom would oversee their own sector. The city of 180,000 people was situated on a coastal bay, and on a clear day one might see the mountains of Spain. Often, the shrill chorus of cicadas could be heard humming in the streets. The poverty was worse than in Mexico, and life was even less expensive. The poor existed on the outskirts of the city in ramshackle slums and provisional dwellings, tin shacks made of pressed oil containers, cardboard, and rags. There was no sewage, potable water, or electricity, and no system of taxation. As a result, only one of ten children received an education, and young ones played in filth in the gutters. Burroughs thought Tangier had an end of the world feeling.

Burroughs found a room for 50 cents a day in a male brothel in the *Medina*, the Arab quarter, where he could get a meal for another quarter, and opiates were easily available over the counter in pharmacies. The streets were crowded with beggars, Berber women bent under loads of charcoal, men on mules and others in white *djellabas*. He met a series of seedy European and American expatriates, many of them to be bizarrely distorted in *Naked Lunch*, as Burroughs would exponentially magnify the French tradition of *roman-à-clef* and raise it to a new level of nightmare.

Soon after his arrival in Tangier, he began writing an uncontrollable outpouring of disconnected sketches—what he called "routines"—weirdly humorous, fantastic elaborations exaggerating the tall-tale tradition previously exploited in a more deadpan voice by Americans like Ambrose Bierce or Mark Twain.

He sent the first of these—the "talking asshole" routine—to Ginsberg. It told a story about a circus ventriloquist who teaches his rectum to talk. The rectum soon assumes a hilarious degree of autonomy, talking incessantly and crying, shouting out in the street its demands for equal rights, using insult, boasting, vilification, and outrageous hyperbole to assert its independence.

Burroughs began injecting cocaine—it made his mind carom like a "berserk pinball machine," he admitted in a letter. He was using heroin excessively and, to reduce his dependence, he began injecting Eukodol, an analgesic and hypnotic morphine substitute. It induced bursts of euphoria, but the Eukodol proved more powerful as an addictive substance than the heroin. He wrote Ginsberg that he feared fuses in his brain would overcharge and blow, allowing black, sooty blood to pour out of his eyes. He was also afflicted by a series of illnesses: rheumatic fever, uremia, and an ankle infection. A German doctor who treated him for these ailments, as well as his addiction, was soon reflected in another recurrent routine about a surgeon who practiced "technological medicine." Dr. Benway was an expert in brainwashing and what Burroughs called biocontrol, which he defined in *Naked Lunch* as "control of physical movement, mental processes, emotional reactions and *apparent* sensory impressions by means of bioelectric signals injected into the nervous system of the subject."

Benway's own cocaine use and botched operations—using a toilet plunger in a heart resuscitation with a bathroom as an operating theater—were pure parody of the notion of a control which, in Burroughs' view, was the primary ambition of the political state, and which he saw as the ultimate addiction. For Burroughs, Benway represented the excesses of absolute authority and the potentially dehumanizing capacity of scientific knowledge used to wield overwhelming power.

Burroughs was sending these routines in letters to Ginsberg and, in March of 1954, complained that he needed to discover a "complete new approach" for their use in fiction. By June, he was wondering whether the letters themselves could be the basis for the book he wanted to write. Calling Tangier "Interzone," Burroughs realized that he might be able to present a series of these routines, where a dream dimension could assume as much significance as any more empiric measurement of reality. While the routines would be unconnected by narrative threads, they would be explosive in themselves and all based on his impressions. In a letter to Ginsberg in early January of 1955, he said this arrangement could discard the "novelistic pretext of dealing directly with his characters and situations."

"Every writer of fiction," Burroughs once observed, "though he may not adopt the dramatic form, writes in effect for the stage."

As his work proceeded, many of the routines evolved into what the critic, Ian MacFadyen, has characterized as "performative monologues." The hybrid discourse of the voices of recurring characters, like Benway, reference each other, parody each other's mannerisms and ideas with an often anarchic unpredictability, incorporating such disparate spheres as advertisements, popular songs, legal and psychoanalytical jargon, and ranting racist and evangelical radio broadcasts which would be cut and spliced and reinserted into the manuscript. The result, MacFadyen observes, is more like a revolving turntable, a whirlwind farce wilder than any novel since *Tristram Shandy*. Such a fluidly cinematic structure would radically depart from the traditional means that novelists had used for several centuries and become one of the precursors of what is now called post-modernism.

Writers like E.M. Forster in *A Passage to India*, Malcolm Lowry in *Under the Volcano,* or Paul Bowles in *The Sheltering Sky* often dramatize a clash and possible merging of a colonialist or foreign visitor's set of values with those of an indigenous people. One side of the transnational basis of *Naked Lunch* is the extent to which the political turbulence of Morocco in the 1950s registers in his depiction of the "nationalist martyrs with grenades up the ass" who "mingle with the assembled conferents and suddenly explode" or Arab rioters throwing burning gasoline on garbage dumps, cutting off heads, "yip and howl, castrating, disemboweling." Such expressions of the violent excesses that can result from pent up revolutionary rage would play a part in the war for independence. The tension between westerners and North Africans was quite palpable in Tangier and made Burroughs carry a six-inch switchblade as protection.

The details of street pandemonium fit in with the hysterical rhythms of *Naked Lunch*, but they are presented in the composite and kaleidoscopic mix of a mosaic presentation that makes the novel so difficult to decipher. Burroughs freely fuses moments recovered from places as disparate as New York City, South America, and Tangier with a bewildering dissonance. On one page, his character, Lee, may be running from detectives on the subway in Queens and, without transition, a boy may be crushing

The Triumvirate

a centipede's head in Mexico City. The travel writer's notion of place is ruptured in Burroughs' more futuristic, caricatured world, affected more by fantasy and surrealistic juxtaposition than memory, realistic detail, or developed characters.

By the fall of 1956 Burroughs had completed a body of work—the words coming to him like dictation, he wrote Ginsberg—but it all seemed endless and without pattern. He had moved to a hotel and was visited by Paul Bowles who lived in Tangier:

> He lived in a damp little room opened into the garden of the Hotel Villa Muniria. One wall of the room, his shooting gallery, was pockmarked with bullet holes. Another wall was completely covered with snapshots, most of which he had taken on a trip to the headwaters of the Amazon.

Burroughs' writing table was chaotic, Bowles remembered, and the floor was littered with various sections of manuscript. At that point, Burroughs was using a hashish candy confection called *majoun* that he would chew on an empty stomach after an hour of vigorous rowing, standing up Venetian style in the choppy waters of the bay. Later in the day, he would smoke joints of marijuana and consume prodigious quantities of alcohol.

Burroughs could not at first imagine how to make all the material he had completed cohere: "It is extremely painful trying to weld all this scattered material," he wrote to Ginsberg. In the spring of 1957, he invited Jack Kerouac and Allen Ginsberg to join him in Tangier, which is when Kerouac retyped much of the manuscript. Bowles remembered the flavor of the collaboration that ensued with his usual charm:

> [Ginsberg] and Bill used to sit around half the night having endless fights about literature and aesthetics. It was always Bill who attacked intellect from all sides, which I suspect was exactly what Allen wanted to hear. . . . as Bill

> stumbled from one side of the room to another, shouting in his cowboy voice, stirring his drink around and around without stopping . . . and with two or three *Kif* cigarettes lighted simultaneously but lying in different ashtrays which he visited on his way around the room.

The collaborative element in all of Burroughs' fiction, starting with *Naked Lunch*, may be another aspect of its transnational character, and later, in Paris and London, more like a film director than a novelist, he would recruit the assistance of friends like the painter Brion Gysin, who gave him the idea for the cut-up method in assembling his manuscripts.

The final order for Naked *Lunch* would be discovered in another hotel room in Paris a year later when Burroughs and an editor named Sinclair Beiles, who was working for the publisher Maurice Girodias, formed its organization with the spontaneity of Marcel Duchamp and a considerable element of accident. Burroughs' anti-novel was presented in a manner no reader had previously encountered, and its commercial availability would have to be validated by judicial process.

The trial was conducted in Massachusetts, which began as the colonial outpost of the seventeenth century Puritans, who had created a harsh theocratic governance that controlled all cultural activity. The dissenting opinion of Justice Paul Reardon was that he had found the novel to be "a revolting miasma of unrelieved perversion" and he certainly would not have been pleased by lines like "we see God through our assholes in the flashbulb of orgasm." However, the majority of the Massachusetts Supreme Court decided that, even if the novel was obscene, it had enough redemptive social value to permit publication.

One of the witnesses for the defense, the novelist Norman Mailer, had testified that Burroughs might be "the most talented writer in America" and later declared that Burroughs was "possessed by genius." Mailer chose the right word, though, like Hemingway, he was usually reluctant to praise other writers whom he regarded as competitors. He probably would have agreed with the critic Walter Benjamin's remark that every great work dissolves a genre or founds a new one. It is a perception that anticipates *Naked Lunch* and explains the difficulty its readers face.

III. Sadhus and Lepers on the Ganges

American authors may be more susceptible to transnational states of mind, since the United States for several hundred years had been ethnically and racially heterogeneous, with an influx of people from all over the planet, some of them conveyed against their wills. More than in any other nation, perhaps, its language broadened, enriched by inclusion of many of the words and cultural principles brought by the newcomers.

In the early spring of 1962, Ginsberg and his companion, Peter Orlovsky, took a boat to India. They would spend a year in Calcutta and the holy city of Benares. *Indian Journals*, the account of Ginsberg's wandering, is drawn from notebook entries of reflections, dreams, inchoate poems, notes on prosody, letters to friends, like Jack Kerouac and Gary Snyder, prodigious reading lists, lists of the dictators supported by the U.S. since World War II and its international political antagonisms, and more sustained observation of what he saw. The book is planetary in outlook though focused on minute particulars.

Ginsberg was thirty-six and he felt he had already consumed half his life span. In his passage to India, he embarked on a vision quest, a search for continued meaning: "What's to be done with my life that has lost its idea?" He realized how much of his previous life had been devoted to the exploration of mind and an alternate consciousness reached through drugs, and how "sad & futile I felt now that I had gotten to the point with hallucinogens where I no longer liked what I felt & was too disturbed & frightened to continue."

Life often proceeds as process more than plan and one of his first observations in Calcutta is inside a Chinese opium den, a dais on a raised platform with a coconut oil lamp. A Chinese man reclined on his hip on a square, worn, thin piece of black leather. He passed to Ginsberg a two-foot, brown, polished bamboo pipe with a bone mouthpiece and a hexagonal metal bowl edged with silver. In the pit of the bowl was a hole in which the pellet of opium was poked and smoked. Unlike eating opium or injecting morphine, the result was a "hypnogogic reverie—long delicious pleasure—an assured constancy of imagination and repose." The scene will recur with variations along the way.

The travelers stay in inexpensive hotels and they celebrate Orlovsky's birthday with a festive dinner of fish and pork noodle soup, eggplant, and prawns for a total of forty-four cents. Street life is a source of constant animation and surprise: trolleys and rickshaws with clanging bells, begging lepers with missing limbs, betel-nut sellers crouching in their booths, people who seem dressed only in underwear, walking in shorts open to the genitals. There are houses filled with hermaphrodites, and on other streets, cots occupied by middle-aged rouged transvestites. He saw barefoot singers whirling, their piercing falsetto sounds echoing repeatedly until they begin to shake as in an epileptic fit. The night suggests miraculous transformations and he sees a dancer who seemed to fly across a stage, "his feet fluttered flat on the ground like pogo sticks a dozen times a second."

On many other nights, Ginsberg is drawn to the great Ganges River where the bodies of the dead are piled on wood and ignited. There are squatting families ringed around devotional flowers and incense, passing pipes of marijuana—called ganja in India, after the river itself. The air has an acrid smell of burning flesh. A blind beggar sang constantly beating a drum while a *sadhu*, a holy wanderer, danced around with "with snaky sex gestures like a burlesque act." At midnight he joins a circle of *sadhus* sitting cross-legged with pipes of ganja, listening to cymbals and drums, watching two men, dressed in women's veils and saris, spinning like dervishes with pumping pelvises.

On one of his last nights in Calcutta, he sits on a blanket with a chanting *sadhu*, his hair braided into a top-knot with red ribbon, a big cow with a third eye painted in red, sharing the

The Triumvirate

space. Ezra Pound never saw India, Ginsberg reflects, and what would his father, Louis Ginsberg, think of him sitting in the dirt with the *sadhus*, smoking in a country where stone statues of giant phallic lingams are worshipped? Just before he leaves Calcutta for Benares, another memory of what he had left behind occurs when he reads the "Insane Genius" *Newsweek* review of *Naked Lunch*.

Ginsberg and Orlovsky take the midnight train to Benares, traveling third class to the oldest continually inhabited city in the world. All night, lurching on the tracks, Ginsberg reads Celine's *Journey to the End of Night* in the dim light. In Benares, they find a stone room with a slate black tile floor near the burning *ghats* for a cost of two dollars a week. The room is quite bare except for a desk, a few straw floor mats, and a rope cot. It has French doors leading to a thirty foot balcony protected by chicken wire to prevent entry by the monkeys, who are often clever enough to find a way in to steal a banana.

On a diet of Mayakovsky and a shot of morphine, he is drawn by the spectacle of Benares at dawn: an old crone with long wild hair rocking back and forth on her haunches wailing, beggars counting beads under burlap, circling rickshaws, women wrapped in shawls carrying brass water pots to the Ganges or flowers to adorn the lingam in the temple overlooking the river. The naked bathers are without self-consciousness in the holy waters next to the charred, still smoking corpses on embers, contrasting elements in the picture. The present is a sufficient subject, he concludes, like Cezanne, he thinks, turning his head an inch as the composition changes.

Ginsberg would spend the next six months in Benares, taking snapshots with his camera, saturated with his own fascination and his diary notations become what he remembers of his dreams and long prose poem notations of what he has seen. The result is an unusual degree of cultural absorption, a dimension so much deeper than that afforded to the sheltered tourist, a rare penetration and access to values and behavior so different from conditioned expectations. The impact would be subsequently measurable in his poetry.

IV. Clues

There are many more clues to the transnationalism of the Beats, from the multiculturalism that came so naturally to so many of them in the early 1950s—see Kerouac's *The Subterraneans*—to the poet Gary Snyder's decade in Kyoto studying the practice of Zen as an acolyte in the Shōkoku-ji temple. John Lennon's comment that his group chose their mysterious, but charming, name in tribute to the Beats is another harbinger.

When I taught at the Sorbonne, in 1982, taking the metro to the university, I saw on four different occasions young people reading *Sur la Route*. In this connection, I was struck when a few years ago, in *The New Yorker*, the Bosnian-American writer, Aleksandar Hemon, explained that he had immigrated to the United States because he thought "it might be fun to Kerouac about in America for a while." A writer's name used as a verb or an adjective is a sign of spreading significance, at least among contemporaries.

One might cite the expulsion of Allen Ginsberg by the Communist puppet government of Czechoslovakia in 1965, after thousands of Czech students had crowned Ginsberg as *Kral Majales*, King of May, to demonstrate influence, or consider the impact of Kerouac on a subsequent generation of musicians like Bob Dylan, Tom Waits, or Leonard Cohen, or writers like Ken Kesey, Thomas Pynchon, or Hunter S. Thompson. In a larger context, one may encounter multiple references to Kerouac, Burroughs, and Ginsberg in Roberto Bolaño's *The Savage Detectives* or *2066,* and such an accounting among contemporary world authors could blossom into a dissertation.

Ginsberg understood that the appeal of the Beats was international and his constant travels abroad became a means by which to disseminate a consciousness that questioned all political and cultural boundaries. Such messages had particular appeal for young people and there were vital centers of interest

The Triumvirate

in cities like Mexico City, Buenos Aires, Calcutta, Heidelberg, Amsterdam, and Paris. Surely, the fact that Kerouac, Ginsberg, and Burroughs have each been translated into over twenty languages is a sign of broad transnational appeal.

IV
Messengers

Bonnie Bremser's Mexico

> The little boy with head fulla water and club foot to boot, the classic cripple on our block, Mexico is full of cripples, the little boy runs loose and teases us, evil crow voice full of croak and guttural sounds echoing the empty space . . . trumpeting the call for all mongrel dogs to come from their nest to greet gringos . . .
>
> *For Love of Ray*

One of the prevalent myths about the Beats is the legend of the all-boy gang, supposedly consisting of Lucian Carr, Allen Ginsberg, Jack Kerouac, and Burroughs cavorting during wartime Manhattan. This frivolous view of hedonism gone wild, of boyish irresponsibility, was perpetuated recently in Hollywood's adaptation of *On the Road*, a film characterized by Kristen Stewart's sex squeals of porcine delight, and another film that focused on the Carr murder, *Kill Your Darlings*.

What actually held the Beats together was their interest in each other's potential to write down the stories of their lives. As has been made apparent by the work of scholars like Nancy Grace and Ronna Johnson, there were a few articulate women in the mix, like the novelist Joyce Johnson and the poets Hettie Cohen, Joanne Kyger, Diane Di Prima, and Anne Waldman. The solid evidence of female participation in the Beat story is provided in two extraordinary memoirs, Johnson's *Minor Characters* and Cohen's *How I Became Hettie Jones*, as well as perhaps the less effective ones by two of Kerouac's recriminating former wives, Edie Parker and Joan Haverty.

Bonnie Bremser is one of the lesser known female figures in the Beat Generation, perhaps because she has written so little, although her personal story is so much more sensational than that of any of the women I have mentioned. She was part of the generation that responded to *On the Road* not long after it was published in 1957 and immediately "felt something was happening and wanted to be a part of it." In March, 1959, at the age of twenty, then called by her maiden name of Brenda Frazer and attending Sweet Briar College, this essentially shy, well-bred woman impulsively married a charmer named Ray, just weeks after meeting him at a poetry reading in Washington. D.C. Ray Bremser preferred calling his new bride Bonnie, and the cheerful glow associated with that Scottish name became an ironic lodestone, a sort of clanging warning of the despair before her.

Bremser was a drinking buddy of Kerouac's, a poet who had been convicted of armed robbery. Like Carolyn Cassady, a judge's daughter with a degree in theater from Bennington College, who fell for the renegade lover Neal Cassady, Brenda Frazer was a privileged child of a Labor Department official who had grown up in affluence and was drawn to her class opposite. Six months after the wedding, Ray was charged with a violation of his parole conditions and the couple fled to Mexico with their infant daughter, Rachel. Their sad story became a sort of Bonnie and Clyde honeymoon in hell.

The act of flight was beat in its spontaneity, perhaps, and like so many of the characters in *On the Road*, Bonnie and Ray were running from something that seemed too confining. The notion, also perhaps in the proper Beat spirit, was improvised and somewhat improvident, and as soon as the couple ran out of money, Bonnie faced a sobering realization: "In Mexico it was nothing but me and the general public between us and starvation and the jailhouse."

In Veracruz, they find a yellow, stucco house, whose inside walls are also plastered with yellow stucco as if the contractor had a happy surplus of material. Their rent, they later learn, is twice the going rate because they are Americans. Bonnie spends six months learning the craft of the street hooker and the bar hustler, and Ray assists in recruiting customers by going to the center of town himself with a photograph of her in a bikini. A pretty, young, blonde American girl is a marketable commodity anywhere, but particularly in Mexico. The meaning of "Veracruz" is true cross she tells us, and this information surely is pertinent. Quaintly—or is it a sign of denial?—she imagines her new calling as going out on "dates," and righteously admits that at times she is "ashamed at enjoying what I am paid for." Sometimes, she is cheated and serves without payment, often it isn't enough to pay for the food or diapers her daughter needs. In general, she cannot understand how Mexicans can live on so little money.

It is as if one of the prostitutes Whitman welcomes as part of his audience (in a snub to the elitism of the poetry world in the Victorian era) or a spokesperson of the mad generation described in "Howl," one of Ginsberg's recklessly self-destructive protagonists, was recounting her misadventures. At one point an older sister visits and Bonnie steals her ring, and then justifies her theft as Burroughs might: "isn't capitalism a big steal in reality?"

Whether capitalism is or isn't a con is not so much the question as Bonnie's exploitation of her own allures as her capital. When she decides she cannot earn enough to pay the bills in Veracruz, she goes on a ten-day jaunt to Mexico City. She complains in a letter to Ray that it rains for three hours each evening and that her feet are bruised from cruising for customers. Although the attempt to tell this sort of story is revolutionary, the narrative becomes a bit tiresome for the readers: one stereotyped, paunchy client after another, most of whom have puny sexual members. With an insistence that causes a little disbelief in the narrative—is it displaced wish fulfillment—too many of these worn out men seem too eager to please her. She suspects many of her clients are repressed homosexuals. Somehow, she is just able to bear the weight of all these strange men bearing down on her. Still, she can't wait until she has earned what she needs in order to return to her baby and her husband.

With a literary touch, she admits she is reading de Sade's *Justine* in her hotel room before going to sleep, but unlike the Marquis, she isn't able to provide the details of the encounters, to relish or disparage the sensations of pleasure or pain, humiliation or conquest that are implicitly available in the situation. In his wickedly unrestrained depictions of carnal manipulation, seduction, and abuse, de Sade has a society and its values to explore and expose. De Sade, of course, like the later *Story of O*, is porn with a redeeming social purpose and a philosophical perspective. *For Love of Ray* has much less dimension, is much flatter, the details of appearance, smell, touch are mostly absent—as if this nightmare of her drudgery never occurred. She seems inured to the terms of her condition. The sexual episodes are not robotic but certainly become routine, almost boring, without the salient edge of danger in de Sade. Bremser's memoir was originally called *Troia*, which is slang French for whore or adventuress, and its narrative consists primarily of one sexual submission after another. Its effect on the reader is burdensome, like an abstracted weight that keeps increasing but which isn't presented with sufficient detail, clarity, or insight.

On her tenth day in Mexico City, her afternoon is spent on an office carpet servicing an attorney who has already become a regular client. He invites her to dinner just to have fun, and after a lot of brandy she is introduced to his two friends. The three men drive her to a party in which she will be shared, *seriatim*, by these three men, who deposit her back at her hotel when they are done and only pay her half the promised amount after she insists on some compensation.

She takes the bus back to Veracruz the next day, and

when she arrives at the stucco house she finds a note under the door from Ray that hits the reader with the brutal impact of a detonation. Weary and bewildered, Ray has been apprehended by police on a drug charge, arrested because of an expired tourist visa, and deported to Laredo, Texas to be held on a fugitive warrant for unlawful flight. The "vulture is already sitting on my shoulder" she writes melodramatically, an image Burroughs uses with more *sang-froid* in the ominous beginning of *Naked Lunch* to signify the dangers Mexico can present when the American is seen as prey.

Most of *For Love of Ray* was written over the next six months as letters to Ray in jail in Texas. The epistolary form is one of the most natural prose forms, but Bremser is handicapped by inadequate training and skill. "Lack of literary experience," she stridently maintains, "means nothing, there is something important to say and it will out and I won't miss any opportunity to call back the pain and put the blame where it should lie." Although the book is full of the raw power of her pain, with something like the anguish one feels reading Herbert Huncke's *Guilty of Everything,* Bremser as a writer can be fuzzy or impressionistic.

She is using Benzedrine and heroin, but isn't able to quite identify these experiences or explore their effects as Burroughs does in *Junky*. Her experiences tend to be jumbled, and she frequently flashes forward or sideways in her chronology. "Everything has taken place on the go," she tells us, sounding like Dean Moriarty in rationalizing his random and inconsiderate actions in *On the Road,* "the screeching terror of speed of everything falling out from underneath you." Then, with an obviousness that betrays her inexperience as a writer, she offers her recurrent dream of bridges collapsing as she plunges into rushing water, "knowing what it is to fall for the last time forever." That "forever" may, indeed, be as overwritten as anything in Thomas Wolfe. Yet, the quality of her suffering is so compelling and intense—despite the blurring which reminds me a bit of Djuna Barnes' *Nightwood*—and the reader is drawn into her narrative. The psychoanalytical question is whether the blur compensates for what cannot be confronted more directly, or measured more analytically?

In a 1999 interview, Bremser declared that she was trying to be influenced by Kerouac, reading him as she was writing her book, listening to jazz as she wrote:

> And I do still think of him as a wonder of the literary world. He had the knack of the long sentence which is carried by an emotional weight fueled by transcendent flashes of realization.

Feminist critics have compared her velocity to Kerouac's, though the rush of her associations is more jagged, more disjointed, without the rhythm that unifies Kerouac's flow.

"Salvage what you can," she advises early on in *For Love of Ray*, "when there is no hope run for your life." This is exactly what she does, but without Rachel, whom she leaves with Jovita, an overweight Mexican surrogate mother figure, who promises to care for her. At the same time, she fears Jovita may want to keep her white daughter. She dyes her hair black and goes to the Mexican border, a sixteen hour bus trip from Veracruz, and finds a weird letter from Ray demanding she share the details of her current sexual activity—he wants her to chart "the several hundred coition points possible in a twelve hour symphony." The incongruity of the letter is reminiscent of some of Henry Miller's ribald characters in *Tropic of Cancer*. It is a twisted love letter of sorts though and at the end of it Ray enjoins her to "make your flesh delirious for me."

Traveling like a tornado, she writes, she screws a Mexican border policeman in Nuevo Laredo, who buys her a dinner of roast goat and tortillas and escorts her across the border to Laredo. The small Texas town is a horror of cheap department stores dominated by federal style government buildings, customs, post office, courthouse, and police. After a brief visit to Ray, she decides to walk beneath his window in "hopeful ritual circles" only to get followed back to her hotel by a police car. What she feels, inchoately perhaps but predictive, reflects the tensions and poisoned politics that exist to this moment and have grown more alarming:

> Border town ballyhoo-sounds of the Rio Grande night, slap of water against the wetback thigh, two nations are at war, the border patrol has antennas and cruises the river marsh bank for the smell of marijuana plants grown from seeds lost from an immigrant pocket. The cop atmosphere here is unbearable. I see persecution as I never knew it existed.

She goes back to Veracruz, another sixteen-hour bus ride, to retrieve her daughter and plead for assistance from the American Consul in Veracruz, who is unsympathetic. Her account seems fictionalized, or at least grossly exaggerated. Full of bitter loathing, she undiplomatically exits his office while spitting on his doorstep and calling his wife a whore. Gathering Ray's poetry manuscripts, she uses all her remaining money to hire a taxi driver to bring her to Mexico City to try to renew her own visa. Hours after a vain bureaucratic shuffle, she only gets an extension.

Some friends in Mexico City help her with enough money to go back to Laredo. She prefers to live in a hotel—a concrete box—on the Mexican side where she can hustle with less fear of prosecution than on the American side. The Mexicans in Nuevo Laredo are different from Veracruz, she observes, more homogenized by the American image. She is allowed to visit Ray twice a week a week, and she walks several miles to the jail with Rachel in her arms. The August heat is unbearable as it radiates off the pavement. The visits are brief; she has to bring food because the Mexican guards eat the best of the prisoner's rations. She can only speak to Ray through a window opening to a holding cell for prison visits. Outside the jail, when she continues to shout to Ray standing at his barred window above, the police threaten to incarcerate her and place Rachel in an orphanage.

Her despair seeps through the pages, her weapons have become silence and contempt, but she has thoughts of suicide. She finds an attorney and a bail bond is arranged. At the same time she signs papers so Rachel can be adopted by a wealthy couple. Whether the adoption is related to the sudden availability of bail funds is unclear, part of the fog of the presentation, but the implication is there. Many years later, Bonnie Bremser would send a letter to *The Village Voice* in New York. She had a complaint about a piece that had appeared in June of 1989 called "The Beat Queens." Her succinct letter appeared on September 7th and reads as follows:

> I would like for you to get the horrible details straight. I did not sell Rachel.
> I gave her for adoption to a couple who wanted to be a family but couldn't have children. There was no money involved. The money came from patrons of the arts in Ft. Worth and was likewise freely given; that's where the getaway money came from.

If *For Love of Ray* resembles *On the Road,* it is because, in both works, movement is zigzag, episodic, sometimes seemingly unprovoked, perpetual, an illustration of mindlessness as Burroughs once famously put it. Unable to face the prospect that at some point Ray may have to return to New Jersey to face the judicial process, they flee again to Mexico to spend the next four months on the trail of mushrooms in the state of Oaxaca. In the mountain town of Huautla, they buy a shoebox full of withered, brownish, black mushrooms, the heads like dried flowers. The two pounds cost five dollars, enough for a permanent high for the next few months. Although the high is ecstatic, the inevitable descent doesn't prevent an increasing edginess, a nervous irritability. They begin to lurch around southern Mexico, apprehensive about the dangers of being rearrested, quarrels escalate into blows, and they become paranoid enough to abandon possessions in hotel rooms.

Most of their travel is by bus, as they fear the vulnerability of hitchhiking.

Whenever their funds are depleted, Bonnie returns to Mexico City. She has bleached blonde hair again and wears perennial sunglasses to ply her trade, leaving Ray to work on his poems. She is unhappy in her work, and reveals, in an aside, her "outlaw scene" of brandishing a knife, demanding her money from a withholding pimp. They decide they have to remain in Mexico City when Bonnie is booked by several regular clients. Her life becomes such an unknowing daze that she is unaware that she is two months pregnant when she has an abortion and her first shot of morphine.

Unlike Emile Zola's groundbreaking novel *Nana*, where the hooker, subservient to the Victorian code of the nineteenth century, succumbs to syphilis, or Theodore Dreiser's *Sister Carrie*, where the prostitute becomes a successful real estate entrepreneur, *For Love of Ray* ends unconvincingly. A New York reporter sends Ray a letter with inaccurate information that charges have been dropped, persuading him to return to serve six months working in the stockroom of Rahway Prison in New Jersey. Bonnie encourages him to face whatever was proposed rather than continue a life on the run. Bonnie receives money from her father and also returns to New York, where on the last page of the book she meets Ray, serendipitously, on a Greenwich Village corner. Ray has been released and is appearing in poetry readings in bars and coffeehouses. As in some implausible fable, the final words of *For Love of Ray* reveal the couple will resume their life together.

The ending seems like an unbelievable *deus ex machina*, a theatrical prop to curtail the narrative in midstream. Like a lot of lurid fiction, the story suddenly runs out of energy and imagination. The tale of horror turns into one of rescue by the faery prince. The problem is that, while memoirs can be successfully merged into hybrid relationships with literary criticism or anthropological observation, the joining of memoir and make-believe usually causes the narrative to be less believable. William James' "willing suspension of belief" becomes too difficult to sustain under such circumstances. The reader may be left with the sour taste of reconfigured experience.

The Beats, as a group, welcomed the writer who had not been trained by the academy, but instead came from the streets, like the poet Jack Micheline, the storyteller Herbert Huncke, or Neal Cassady, the railroad brakeman who read Proust. Bonnie Bremser's story can be appreciated in that context and it comes down to us as an authentic beat journey to the underworld, though grimier, more gritty and sordid than the gymnastics displayed by the members of Ginsberg's "mad generation" in "Howl" or Kerouac's in *On the Road*. The world of Burroughs' *Junky*, as devoid of sentiment as it is, comes closer, though its pain is always more sharply articulated.

For me, this points to the real deficiency of *For Love of Ray*. The excess of her story, the exploits of her sexual service, becomes somewhat numbing to the reader when he or she discovers that there is little else to the narrative. She isn't the kind of writer who can articulate sensations as they occur, but instead barrages the reader with a slew of incidents that seem more or less the same because she doesn't really see distinctions. Lacking the sensuous grasp of detail any reader needs to feel the situation, she bares it without evaluation. While there is something very beat about such an unadorned presentation—Burroughs says the naked lunch is what you see on the end of your fork—it may leave readers at a loss for explanation. Bremser says, about her work as a prostitute, that she always approached it as an amateur, a naïve unprofessional, never as a calculating seductress. She is that kind of writer as well.

Bonnie's reunion with Ray may have provided a fortune cookie ending, but the reunion didn't last. She eventually got an M.A. in soil science, worked for the Department of Agriculture, and had a dairy farm. I never met Bonnie Bremser, though I did have a revealing encounter with Ray Bremser in Boulder, Colorado in 1982. Ginsberg had invited me there to participate in the gathering he had organized at Naropa and the University of Colorado, to commemorate the twenty-fifth anniversary of the publication of *On the Road*. I had written a screenplay for what would become the first film on Kerouac and was intent on interviewing as many people as I could who had known him.

I knew Bremser had written much of his first book, *Poems of Madness*, in a jail cell, and a tribute to Bonnie, *Angel*, on light brown toilet paper in another cell. It was a poem, he said, written in one dark night of solitary confinement. Like Neal Cassady or Gregory Corso, Bremser epitomized the fast-talking, rollicking, street hipster, con-man reckless abandon that Kerouac romanticized with the depiction of Dean in *On the Road* and the glorious exploding roman candle image for madness early in the novel.

Bremser was especially edgy and surly when I met him, full of a coiling tension I found disconcerting. Perhaps the presence of the sound technician and cameraman, who were setting up to film our interview made him suspicious. Ginsberg had persuaded him to meet me, but he did not seem to understand my purposes. Maybe he had quickly sized me up as if I was an F.B.I. informant? I recognized his fear because I had tried to interview people like Lucian Carr and Herbert Huncke, men who had been incarcerated and were inevitably changed by the severity of the experience, and forever distrustful of people who asked too many questions.

Bremser and I were seated in director's chairs on a lawn and, as Bremser nervously crossed his legs, I noticed a bulge in his glossy high leather boot. I asked him about it as a small-talk means of relaxing him. Turning almost cheerful, he pulled a stick of dynamite out of his boot, waving it in the air defiantly, and, leering at me, he explained that western miners provisioned themselves in this manner because they used explosives in their work. Then he pointed the eight inch long red cylinder at my face and exclaimed, with a manic gleam in his eyes, that the dynamite could be used for claim jumpers as well. My guess is that I represented the claim jumper, the historian who wanted to know what actually happened and why it occurred. Bremser's aura of unpredictable irresponsibility was intimidating, so I abruptly discontinued the interview. But it made me understand how much Bonnie had dealt with.

Judith Malina
at the Barricades

I. Moon Magic

> "who distributed Supercommunist pamphlets in Union Square weeping and undressing while the sirens of Los Alamos wailed them down, and wailed down Wall, and the Staten Island ferry also wailed,"
>
>   Lines alluding to The Living Theatre
>   from Allen Ginsberg's "Howl"

In 1945, nineteen-year-old Judith Malina auditioned for the famed German director, Erwin Piscator, Brecht's collaborator on "Three Penny Opera." She performed a dance accompanying her own poem, "Lunar Bowels." Shouting, spinning like a gyrating rubber doll, she tried to express being trapped inside the moon while yearning to return to earth:

        voluminous universe

        against my cheek and thigh
        and pain of all space
                against my breast surge
                and then-------
                MOON
        my foot upon the moon
        my foot upon the slippery moon
        moon globular and light
        ungravitated
        `   dance
                and
                          leap
        a hundred feet!

    This is a fragment of a poem that took five minutes to perform and it reveals the jagged, rough ambitions of youth. Her movements on the stage convinced Piscator to allow Judith into his acting program at the New School. She had chosen the moon as her subject, a "moon-child" of sorts then, identifying with its luminescent longing desire and magical potency.

    Her central desire was to build a theatrical community that would speak with the poet's voice to the suffering and injustice in the world. On a shoestring in 1947, with her husband, Julian Beck, she created a theatrical adventure devoted to dramatic experiment, and the most political perspective since Clifford Odets in New York City. Although Julian died in 1986, Judith kept The Living Theatre alive in a subterranean space on the Lower East Side until her recent death, and its embers still glow.

    As with Burroughs, Kerouac, and Ginsberg, Mexico provided the ignition for a sort of conversion experience. On a belated honeymoon with Julian in Mexico City in 1948, Judith was overwhelmed by the grotesque poverty she saw: barefoot beggars, peasants in rags selling religious articles, a man without arms weaving baskets with his toes. The key encounter was in Taxco, the silver town south of Mexico City, when a blind boy, with suppurating sores in place of his eyes, begged for alms. Judith screamed in revulsion, but understood when she returned to New York that the real mission of her theater would be to assist the untouchables of the world.

They began by renting the oldest theater in the city, the Cherry Lane in Greenwich Village on Commerce Street—the street shaped like a horseshoe. Ironically, perhaps, it was the commercial side of theatrical longevity that eluded them. They staged plays by Gertrude Stein, the San Francisco anarchist, and classicist, Kenneth Rexroth, the poet, John Ashbery, and the painter, Pablo Picasso. With extremely limited financial resources, actors were barely paid. Some of them began staying overnight in the theater, causing problems with a landlord who planned to gentrify the area. When the Fire Department declared that Julian's sets—often drawn on brown paper—were flammable, they were ejected. It was the start of a pattern.

Judith was so passionate about her theatrical aspirations that they began performing what they called Chamber Theater for invited guests—some of them the nascent group of Abstract Expressionist painters whom Julian knew—who sat on pillows on the floor of their living room on the upper West Side. They found a loft in their neighborhood, four flights up in a wooden building on Broadway and 100th Street, and began performing plays by Ibsen, Strindberg, and Pirandello that suggested a model for spontaneity and ways to liberate theater for the future.

They charged a modest admission, but would let you in for free if you could not pay. When they put on a play about Socrates by the anarchist Paul Goodman, in which one of the philosopher's students admitted on stage that "our master is fucking me," the space was vacated by the Department of Buildings as unsafe for audiences and unlicensed for theater.

It does sound hard to believe that a single Anglo-Saxon expletive for copulation whispered on a stage could close a theater, but Julian understood that they were living in what he characterized as an ice age of repression in the 1950s. Goodman, a poet and novelist, as well as a playwright, had been fired by three academic institutions for staging plays alluding to homosexuality. He also practiced a kind of psychoanalysis, called gestalt therapy, without a license, and encouraged Judith and Julian down an anarchist/pacifist path in which what one wrote or said should risk dangerous consequences.

Once again, Judith and Julian were without a theatrical space, but they had formed the core of an idealistic community of actors and artists—Bertold Brecht's godchildren—who wanted their work to affect change. Their unprecedented commitment was reflected in the gritty labor of renovating the space they found on 14th Street and Sixth Avenue. It was the beginning of off-off-Broadway theater as the actors themselves, and other volunteers, demolished the former department store's interiors, dragged out the debris, constructed a stage, and then carried in the seats, the bricks, and the plaster needed to rebuild.

One of the volunteers, incidentally, was Carl Solomon, the dedicatee of "Howl." Carl had walked out of Pilgrim State, the psychiatric institution where he spent years, and mysteriously ended up helping during the period of reconstruction. I cite the story only to substantiate the kinship between the Beats and the Living Theatre, their thespian cousins. The initial foundation of the relationship was a high school friendship formed by Jack Kerouac and Julian Beck.

At the repertory they formed on 14th Street, Judith and Julian decided to do plays by unknown Americans, and in 1959 they staged *The Connection*, about a group of anguished addicts in an interminable wait for the man who would bring them heroin. The subject, despite Nelson Algren's *Man with a Golden Arm* and William Burroughs' *Junky*, was taboo as stage entertainment. What proved most exciting to returning audiences was Julian's notion of allowing four jazz musicians to make music on one side of the stage and interact as the play continued. The musicians were Afro-Americans, former addicts who could not get the cabaret licenses required for public performance in New York City because the track marks on their arms made them fail the requisite physical exam.

What finally closed the 14th Street facility, one that was shared at the time by Merce Cunningham, his dancers, and John Cage, was a play called *The Brig,* about abuses in the U.S. Marine penal system. Ken Brown, a Yale graduate, had served in the Marine Core. Stationed in Okinawa, he received a 30-day sentence in the Marine brig for overstaying a recreational pass.

The punishment was harsh and brutal. Prisoners were identified by numbers, had their heads shaved, and were forbidden to speak to each other no matter what the circumstances. Belittled and insulted by the guards, there was a rigid protocol for every step in the prison barracks. Any failure to conform could result in a humiliating strip search or a baton blow to the stomach.

The action of Brown's play was simple, repetitive, and hellish. It showed the progress of a day from sunrise to bedtime, arranging the action in a series of dehumanizing episodes where the excruciatingly boring routine of the prisoners was interrupted by torture from the guards. Influenced by Antonin Artaud's *The Theater and Its Double*, the play was directed by Judith using intense lighting effects and deliberately raising the volume of voices to rouse an audience from the comfortable complacency of being spectators. The effect was shocking. When the play was reviewed in the winter of 1963 by Howard Taubman, the *New York Times* drama critic, he was so appalled by what it portrayed that he demanded a federal investigation.

Instead, the theater was padlocked by agents of the I.R.S. on charges of tax avoidance. The Living Theatre was a legally chartered non-profit, although the charge was based on failure to pay the I.R.S. *in full* the withholding taxes on the miniscule actors' salaries. The company insisted on performing and found a way into the theatre. The I.R.S. cut off the power but light was provided by television cameras. Demonstrators were in the street and in the messy end the actors, Judith and Julian, were dragged to paddy wagons.

There was a courthouse trial and absurd histrionics—Judith in a black Portia robe carried up the courthouse steps by Julian. Judith was sentenced to a month in prison and Julian two months. It was the beginning of a diaspora as the members of the company, their spouses and children, fled to Europe where, in Belgium, an aristocratic leftist gave them a place to live and work. They came to Europe with the *success de scandale* of having been censored by a society that supposedly valued free expression, and performed *The Brig* on German television for millions of viewers. Judith, Julian, and the company members collaborated on creating *Mysteries, Frankenstein,* and *Paradise Now,* highly experimental and ritualized performances sometimes closer to dance than traditional drama, which they would stage on sets they often had to build themselves, all over Europe for the next five years.

II. The Moon Entries

Although *Full Moon Stages* is a posthumous publication, Judith fully intended every entry as a signifying sign. It begins in 1964, the beginning of the exile. A literary curiosity, the kind of book only a small, adventurous press would have the courage to publish, it is a minimalist, although touchingly intimate, record of a life of phenomenal activity, as Judith would make a brief hand entry for whatever occurred on every full moon for the next fifty years.

Full Moon Stages is unlike her fuller, more detailed diaries—a lifetime effort begun after Judith met Anaïs Nin. Judith's first diary collection, *The Enormous Despair,* was published by Random House in 1972, and a huge segment covering 1947 to 1957 was published by Grove Press in 1984. Judith's diaries are never as salaciously provocative as Nin's, but more devoted to exploring the emotional consequences of personal love and political struggle. The entries in *Full Moon Stages* are imagined differently as brief notations, haiku blinks in an eventful life.

One of the first entries for 1964 notes that a member of the troupe "went mad in London"—a sign, perhaps of the dangerous leap the company had made with Judith and Julian, but also of the precarious risk involved—of family coherence, career, and national identity. A subsequent entry for the same year bears quotation:

> At the Full Moon in December
> I was in jail in Passaic, New Jersey
> for contempt of court.

Understated, as tersely clipped as Catullus, such messages—like those enigmatic mysteries sometimes found in bottles at the edge of a sea—come with a submerged impact. What she cannot reveal here, due to the formal limitations she accepts, is that she was obligated to return to the U.S. to serve her sentence where, in her cell, her warden ordered her to sew damaged American flags. If she had time, she was able to work on her translation of *Antigone*.

Each of the more than five hundred entries begins like the December entry with, "At the Full Moon in," naming the month in question. A solemn invocation, with its improper capitalization suggesting the ritual and mythic dimension of the event, this simple repetition—as fundamental in its use as in the *Old Testament* or Greek lyric—is the rhythmic basis we soon realize of a poem of life more than an anecdotal memoir. The music of the repetition, its insistent organizing principle, functions like the serial arrangement in Cage, Steve Reich, or Phillip Glass, and it provides a haunting resonance. The impact on a reader over two hundred pages is cumulative. Even though Malina's lens may be tightly focused, the scope of her story stretches over a half-century.

Many of the entries from 1965 through 1972 commemorate the whirlwind of European travel to perform *Mysteries, Frankenstein, Paradise Now,* Jean Genet's *The Maids,* and *Antigone* in Berlin, Frankfort, Milan, Venice, Rome, Amsterdam, Brussels, and Paris, on an American tour in 1968, and also on the edge of the Sahara in Morocco and in a *favela* in Ouro Preto, Brazil. Sometimes life intrudes and there are notes of Seders, the birth of Judith's daughter, Isha, the company battling the flu in France, and acting in a Pasolini film in Italy, or Judith dancing naked under the moon at an outdoor performance.

Some entries, like the one for July, 1971, seem particularly disturbing:

> At the Full Moon in July we were in prison
> In Belo Horizonte DOPS, and Julian's mother
> Came to take Isha out of Brazil.

The generals who ran Brazil had become suspicious of the company's free performances in the slums, and had manufactured a pretext for arrest of the entire company, a sham trial and some selectively applied but brutal torture.

The company returned to the United States, still on the road, performing new work like *The Seven Meditations*, *The Tower*, and *Six Public Acts*, demonstrating against wars and nuclear testing. In one entry, in June of 1971, Judith flatly announces having "made love on the roof with Abbie Hoffman." Do we take such an admission as a sign of revolutionary communion or of the confusing, turbulent despair felt by many that despite all the *sturm und drang* of the 1960s, little real change would occur?

Julian and Judith had two children and an open marriage. In her diaries, she weaves accounts of love affairs with the writer James Agee, the composer Alan Hovhaness, and others. But this rooftop revelation is somehow quite jarring; it appears with the sudden surprise of a flag prematurely declaring victory in the midst of battle. Unlike the more substantial understanding provided in diary entries, this jolts like a flasher's naked display.

In 1976, the company bounced back to Europe, walking in woods in Bavaria on *Walpurgisnacht*, driving to Madrid in their Volkswagen buses for street theater, while surrounded by police, "carrying our bags of Matzos" for a Seder whose service had been written by Judith. With local support, they spent most of the next seven years in Italy.

The itinerant travel continued until a staggering entry in 1984:

> At the Full Moon in June Julian was in the
> Medical Arts Hospital, gravely ill, where
> Allen Ginsberg visits him, is gloomy and takes
> pictures, while Hanon calls everywhere to find
> ahopeful therapy.

Julian would recover sufficiently to perform as a machine-gunning gangster in Francis Ford Coppola's *The Cotton Club* and then in a Beckett play, *That Time*, but would die of cancer in 1985.

Judith had a few startling cameo appearances on television—naked again in *ER*, and clothed in *The Sopranos*. She got roles in several films, in *Awakenings*, then as Anjelika Houston's mother in *The Addams Family*, and yet another mother in *Household Saints*. In 1988, she married Hanon Reznikov, a company member and a gifted playwright who was able to help organize the continuing theatrical commitment in Alphabet City, on Third Street near Avenue C, and then finally in a dank, cavernous underground space on the Lower East Side, on Clinton Street near the Williamsburg Bridge.

Judith's health was compromised by a struggle with lung cancer and in the spring of 2013 she had to give up her theater. She was too ill to manage her affairs any longer and was moved to the Lillian Booth Actor's Home in Englewood, New Jersey. It was no surprise to hear she was unhappy there: for a woman who had led so active a life, the home may have seemed penitential.

III. A Personal Reflection

Judith Malina was committed to her vision of a better world, a thespian agitator for the causes in which she believed. Although theater was her stage, she led her actors as a tribal family into a world of inequality and injustice, where she was often ignored by the silences of the age or rebuffed by authority

I don't believe I've ever met anyone as determined to make her voice heard, and I've rarely come so close to anyone quite so passionate, so brimming with the desire to cause change and affect consciousness.

Antonin Artaud and her teacher, Erwin Piscator, taught her to stress the sincerity of the actor who could become a semaphore in an age of denial. Julian Beck, her first husband, called it the "Ice Age" and the 1950s, when they formed The Living Theatre, was crowded with sleepwalkers. Judith's purpose was to wake audiences with what Valeska Gert, another of Judith's models, called "The Unspeakable Cry!" Whether she was harassed by the agents of legal systems in New York, Europe, or South America, or incarcerated for free expression on a stage, she remained resolute, ready to continue. To the end, she was an ideological warrior of song, dance, and poetry.

Although I had been to the 14th Street theatre in the early 1960s, when I was an undergraduate, to see plays like *The Connection, Many Loves,* and *The Brig,* I got to know her better in the early 1990s, when a poet named Ira Cohen persuaded me to write the history of her theatre. Judith had read my book *Naked Angels* and admired *The Solitary Volcano*, my biography of Ezra Pound.

At that time, most of the Living Theatre's archive was located in a small room off the kitchen in her apartment on West End Avenue and 99th St. The room was a claustrophobic enclosure—called a "maid's room" on the Upper West Side—crammed from floor to ceiling with filing cabinets and boxes. The furniture was sparse: a ladder, a small, rickety, wooden table, an uncomfortable wooden straight-backed chair. The only sign of bourgeois comfort was a collapsed, torn, and weathered recliner. I spent a few years in this dusty room (and never found the maid).

With the intuitive certainty of those who know their work will make a difference, Judith had saved every scrap of Living Theatre history, from newspaper accounts to playbills and post cards. This material is now contained in over three hundred boxes in the Beinecke Collection at Yale University. Judith had also stored in that sprawling apartment all the volumes of the daily diary she had been keeping since she met Anaïs Nin in 1947, and the twenty volumes of journal entries that her husband Julian had written before his death in 1985. Judith was willing to explain the significance of every detail, and my queries often led to ramifications and turns of which I had been unaware.

My method was to slowly examine the archive, reading the journals that corresponded, making my notations. After a few hours of this process, I would sit with Judith in her living room asking for clarification. We were surrounded by Julian's paintings—some hung on the walls, others stacked around the room. I often used a small tape recorder because Judith usually would be smoking marijuana, politely passing the joint to me when she completed her thought. In its way, this became the most stimulating research I would ever experience, an occasion where the flexibility of the mind might lead to fluency and insight.

I saw her last on the margins of Manhattan in her basement theatre on Clinton Street a few years ago, when she sponsored the memorial for Ira Cohen, the poet who had urged me to write her history. She was as responsible and bravely defiant as ever, still anxious about funding, concerned with issues of vitality and relevance, with the plays she was planning to direct, with the importance of keeping alive a theatrical company that could explore dissenting political perspectives, one that could hope to do more than merely entertain.

To reach the Clinton Street location one had to descend a particularly long stairway to a sub-basement that felt as damply oppressive as the subway. It was the exact polar opposite of

Broadway business, where a tourist ticket could cost several hundred dollars, a visa to see the dancing legs of showgirls and the world of culture and "art." Broadway was built by investors; The Living Theatre was always dependent on donations.

    Judith kept her Clinton Street space going until early in 2013. She died at eighty-eight, five days after the Full Moon, in April of 2015, of emphysema. After her burial next to Julian, there was a gathering in her honor at a loft theater on Fourteenth Street, a half a block from where her group had performed *The Connection* and *The Brig*. There were no eulogies, no sanctimonious remarks, no vapid evaluations. I remained for four hours, but when I left, the assembled actors, admirers, and friends of the theatre continued to drink organic wine and converse. It was the salon of the Living Theatre, which is exactly how Judith Malina would have wanted herself remembered.

Patti Smith's Matchbox

> "It's not so easy writing about nothing."
> Patti's dream notation

There has always been something mysterious, enigmatic, baffling for me about Patti Smith. Her image—projected so powerfully in *Just Kids*—is that of the lanky, curious urchin who is not afraid to say "ain't," who can mix the most vernacular immediacy with a more fastidious linguistic elegance. Her songs vibrate to the sensibility of the street, yet the prose in *M Train* seems so deliberately fashioned, poised, calculated, polished. Her world, she explains, comes on "a platter filled with allusions," and the dish she serves is sometimes crowded with them. The discrepancy between the scrappy urchin persona and the story she tells is so dramatic that I've heard malicious gossip of a ghostwriter.

Like the singer, Bruce Springsteen, Smith identifies with exploited working stiffs and the underprivileged, with an urgency that underlines her rhythm. Like Bob Dylan or Neil Young, her sound can twang with a whining, nasal anguish of populist complaint, the expression of an impossible romantic yearning. Sometimes, especially now, her speaking voice can grate like a heel dragging on gravel.

With Tom Waits, she has been connected to a post-Beat

tradition. She refers to the Beats as apostles, and to herself as their orphaned offspring. Admiring William Burroughs, she shares his ambition of exposing the social sham that allows us to rationalize our wasteful consumerism. She remembers visiting Burroughs in *M Train*, watching him shoot target practice. Burroughs was a marksman to the end and, like him, Smith seems to be a straight shooter, which may be why she presents herself to the world unadorned, without the cosmetic covers we expect from celebrity.

Burroughs claimed, in the "Atrophied Preface" to *Naked Lunch*, that his experimental ambition was to write entirely in the present, without memory. *M Train* is a book of memories, and one of the charming stories she tells is of voyaging to Veracruz, Mexico, on Burroughs' recommendation, in search of the perfect cup of coffee. Quite unlike Burroughs, though, she admits to a "fascination with melancholia," which can lead to a sentimentality usually absent from Burroughs' more brutal world.

The beginning of *M Train* is particularly enticing. Smith relates a dream in a café, featuring a laconic cowboy wearing his Stetson pulled down to his eyes, the sun glinting off his belt buckle. Writing in a little pocket notebook, he leans backwards on a folding chair and declares, "It's not so easy writing about nothing." The proposition insinuates the absurd. Writing is an addiction he observes, staring out into tumbleweed desert and white sky. This cowboy seems to have wandered out of a Sam Shepard play—Eddie in "Fool for Love" or the earlier "Cowboy Mouth," performed in its initial production in 1971 by Shepard himself and his lover at that time, Patti Smith. The cowboy in Smith's dream is a prop, an arrogant dramatic tease who flatly advises Smith that she is merely sharing *his* dream. This strange, metaphysical parable ends abruptly with the cowboy's drawling commonplace: "The writer is a conductor." The scene sets the stage for us with characteristic economy and sharp detail.

In fact, the reader immediately is caught in her dream. She wakes and proceeds to the Café 'Ino on Bedford Street in

Greenwich Village for her usual black coffee, toast, and olive oil. Since the early Renaissance, the coffeehouse has been the place where progressive, often revolutionary ideas were exchanged, where a new code of manners could be displayed. With its orange awning, the Café 'Ino, and the quest for black coffee, is an organizing motif in Smith's narrative. She goes there to write, but, staring at the ceiling fans, she worries that "It is not so easy writing about nothing."

Using, as a segue, her own dream of owning a café, she relates the history of a bizarre honeymoon journey she took to Saint-Laurent-du-Maroni, a border town in northwest French Guiana where the French had built a penal colony for the sort of prisoner they hoped would never return to France. In his book, *The Thief's Journal*, Jean Genet had seen this infernal place as hallowed ground, lamenting that he had been incarcerated elsewhere.

In 1981, with her rock guitarist husband, Fred Sonic Smith, she went to Saint-Laurent with the romantic intention of bringing Genet a parcel of its earth and stones. Genet may be considered a literary cousin of William Burroughs', whom Smith had already met, and who promised to assist her in delivering this sacrament.

After flying to Suriname, Patti and Fred cross the Maroni River bordering French Guiana in a dugout canoe. Paddled by a small boy, the trip takes an hour in torrential rain, the river teeming with piranha. It is a bit like crossing the Archeron to Hades. After finding refuge from the rain in a bar, they are escorted to a spartan hotel:

> A small bottle of watered-down cognac and two plastic cups were set on the dresser. Spent, we slept, even as the returning rain beat relentlessly on the corrugated tin roof. There were bowls of coffee waiting for us when we awoke. The morning sun was strong. I left our clothes to dry on the patio. There was a small chameleon melting into the khaki color of

> Fred's shirt. I spread the contents of our pockets on a small table. A wilting map, damp receipts, dismembered fruits, Fred's ever-present guitar picks.

These declarative, short sentences seem as minimal as Catullus' or Hemingway's with the same focused insistence on visible details: cognac, coffee bowls, a chameleon on a khaki shirt. Like Williams' "The Red Wheelbarrow," which focuses with such insistent clarity on the ordinary, the white chickens in the rain we often take for granted, Smith's detail suggests, on face value, what the cowboy has called "nothing." Her sharpened brevity and heightened focus, however, come with an insidious Conradian dimension, ominous, warning somehow. In the ruined prison, a few stray chickens scratch in the dirt around an abandoned bicycle. The bicycle is another sign of incongruity, like Fred's insistence on a shirt and tie despite the tropical heat. In a large dank room, occupied only by scuttling beetles, with heavy rusted chains illuminated by shafts of light, she finds the dirt and stones for Genet and places them in an oversized Gitanes matchbox.

In the town of St. Laurent, where she sees no women, no children playing, or even a dog, they find a man wearing aviator sunglasses and a leopard print shirt who agrees to drive them to Cayenne. Explaining that the trunk of his beaten-up Peugeot is used to transport chickens, they agree to put their bags in the back seat. At a military checkpoint, the car is searched and a man is found curled in the trunk "like a slug in a rusting conch shell." They are interrogated separately at a police station, and though they are ultimately given cognac and released, Smith builds considerable tension into her narrative, the kind of hovering apprehension you might find in Denis Johnson's *The Laughing Monsters*. The honeymoon memory is the most focused part of the book.

The structure of *M Train* is influenced by W.G. Sebald. Its mood is elegiac and reverential, punctuated by reliquaries, ritual, and talismanic signs, and its dominant mode is reverie.

Messengers

Her theme is suggested in a question: "How is it that we never completely comprehend our love for someone until they're gone?" The rapidly shifting memories, from the quest for coffee in the Café 'Ino to childhood, to marriage with Fred Smith, to her strange literary pilgrimages are fluidly organized with a flow of associations more like Heraclitus than Aristotle.

M Train will perplex the conventional reader with its insistence on allowing dreams to speak, on the presence of conversations with inanimate objects. At one point she walks up to the Serbian Orthodox Cathedral in Manhattan and faces the bust of Nikola Tesla, who discovered alternate current. The bust advises her, in the kind of animation only possible in the stupor of a dream, that she has "misplaced joy." Much of the book is a kind of displaced grieving for those she has lost along her way: her parents, Fred Smith, who died in 1994 of a heart attack at the age of 45, her brother Todd of a massive stroke one month later, the artists from whom she learned. These figures recur: images, Smith writes, have a way of dissolving and then abruptly returning, reminders of former joys and pain.

Throughout the book she claims that she is having difficulties with writing and trouble finding a subject. Her problem is perennial for writers: has the well gone dry? The dream shadow of the cowboy reappears periodically—a fabulous invention, a fancy that reminds us that this is also a book about trying to write *something*. She notes his nickel spurs and the snake scar on his collarbone, a crescent moon tattooed in the space between his thumb and forefinger. It is a writer's hand, she concludes, and her numinous "Homeric drifter" offers the usual commonplace advice with an Orphic edge.

She finds inspiration in reading: Bolaño, Murakami, Wittgenstein. She confesses to an inability to remember what she has read, so she rereads. Like Sebald, she includes Polaroid snapshots she takes at Nietzsche's last residence, an oval table in a garden where Goethe and Schiller spent hours conversing, the home of Frida Kahlo, her "secret guide since sixteen," Hesse's typewriter, Beckett's spectacles, the gravesites of Jean Genet, Sylvia Plath, and Rimbaud. Some of the snaps are as blurred as memory.

Smith has been accused of "bookish necrophilia," but the charge seems jealous. The travels for these photos are gracefully, though sometimes elliptically, woven into a narrative that may seem discursive to some, lugubrious, or pretentious even, to others. The more generous among us will appreciate that any artist can find inspiration in her sources.

Memoir focuses on the moments that have been most meaningful, and *M Train* is a marvelous, stately procession of such moments. One of the most poignant of these moments occurs near the end of the book, when she remembers a visit to Paul Bowles, ailing and fragile in Tangiers. Then Smith brings the Gitanes matchbox, with the dirt and stones of Saint-Laurent prison, to Genet's grave. The matchbox had resided in her desk for twenty years, wrapped in one of Fred's handkerchiefs.

V
Artisans and Impresarios

Laughlin's Literary Lost Souls

"Do something useful with your life!"
Ezra Pound to James Laughlin, 1933

James Laughlin was one of the heroes of modern publishing and an avatar of the best in small-press Jeffersonianism. Written with genuine feeling for the material, with a supple, lucid prose, quite free of the "newspeak" of academic jargon, and with a scrupulous documentary insistence, Ian MacNiven's *Literachoor Is My Beat* is the first life of Laughlin, and its narrative is remarkable.

Laughlin had the pedigree formerly associated with British and American publishing. On his maternal side, there were officers who fought in the American Revolution and an ensuing D.A.R. legacy. His father's family, Irish potato farmers, emigrated early in the nineteenth century. There had been a fortunate marriage for the first James Laughlin in 1840 that enabled a career in banking and led to the manufacture of steel in Pittsburgh. The Laughlins consorted, and sometimes married, with Fricks, Carnegies, Mellons, and the millionaire industrial barons of Pittsburgh.

The Laughlin fortune was forged by fabricating the iron rails used to connect America after the Civil War, and by 1900 the Jones & Laughlin Company was the second largest steel producer in the country. Although his father was a playboy, his mother reinforced a strict Calvinist code that left him, as Laughlin put it, with a sense of the "moral responsibility to uplift people and to improve the world."

MacNiven argues that such service may have also been a function of guilt, an expiation of privilege. Laughlin's grandfather had a yacht moored on property he owned in Nantucket, his father drove a fire engine red Pierce-Arrow (his mother had two grey ones), and he was given his own thirty foot yacht at the age of fifteen and a Model A Ford at seventeen. Laughlin was raised in several opulent households, but, to avoid his father's mental decline, he spent a year in the Institut Le Rosey in Switzerland, one of the most exclusive boarding schools in Europe, where all instruction was in French.

His preparatory education continued at Choate where he was near a favorite aunt in Connecticut, and where one of his instructors was Dudley Fitts, a musician, poet, translator, and scholar, who opened the pathway to the modernism of Pound, Eliot, Stein, Joyce, Cummings, and William Carlos Williams. In 1932, he graduated from Choate at the top of his class and chose (despite paternal tears) to go to Harvard, even though Princeton was the usual family destination. T.S. Eliot was the poet-in-residence at Harvard and Laughlin probably audited classes he offered, devoted in part to the poetry of Ezra Pound. When Dudley Fitts (whose influence was similar to Father Cyril Fay's on the young F. Scott Fitzgerald at the Newman School) wrote a letter of introduction to Pound, Laughlin asked whether he could visit Pound in Italy and, famously, Pound's terse, gnomically imagist response from Rapallo was "visibility high."

Pound's exhilarating fulminations on the state of world politics and American writing continued in correspondence, letters written in Pound's spectacular homemade frontier dialect, a peculiar pungently unorthodox flow of invented language and cockeyed orthography. Reminding Laughlin of the importance of American poets, like William Carlos Williams, Pound had become a mentor—the odd title of MacNiven's biography signifies this. Laughlin, writing for *The Harvard Advocate*, got Pound's philippic "Ignite Ignite" printed in the magazine, as well as an essay by Williams. He continued to try to place work by Pound and purchased a used handset press to further that process, but by the end of his second year at Harvard he sailed to Europe for an informal tutorial at what he called the "Ezuversity."

By the fall of 1934 he was in Rapallo, fascinated by what Pound called the "Eddycashun," a digressive exfoliating monologue, delivered mostly at mealtimes, on economics, politics, literary ancients and moderns, all packaged in Pound's slangy, cracker-barrel idiom, his hilarious mimicry of high and low dialects, and his wicked burlesque of class affectations. Pound was quick to offer suggestions for reading. One book that would prove particularly provocative was *Tropic of Cancer*, which Henry Miller had sent to Pound: "a dirty book that's pretty good" was Pound's recommendation.

Ezra Pound—whose motto was Make It New, and whom Laughlin addressed as "Boss"—also advised that Laughlin do something useful in his life. As if steel lacked sufficient utility in the poet's eyes, he told Laughlin to start publishing an annual poetry anthology and gave him a list of writers. This project would evolve into New Directions, the publishing company Laughlin founded with inherited assets. Laughlin had also resumed his studies at Harvard and persuaded his fellow editors on the *Advocate* to include a piece by Pound on religion and a story by Miller. The issue was seized by the Cambridge police with scandalous reports in the Boston and New York papers.

More cautious as a publisher, Laughlin would only publish Miller's non-fiction subsequently. Still, he deserved the reputation of the American publisher who pursued an avant-garde and took the greatest risks: he printed Pound, both William Carlos Williams and Tennessee Williams, crucial novels that otherwise might never have appeared, like Djuna Barnes' *Nightwood* and Paul Bowles' *The Sheltering Sky*, and an abridged version of Jack Kerouac's *Visions of Cody*, when no other American publisher would consider it. Laughlin was particularly interested in the Beats and published an amazing list of contemporary American poets like Gary Snyder, Gregory Corso, and Lawrence Ferlinghetti (whose *Coney Island of the Mind* sold almost a million copies). Furthermore, he commissioned many translations of European writers, like Brecht and Herman Hesse, and of South Americans, like Pablo Neruda and Borges, a continuing commitment that helped to diminish American provincialism and insularity. Such efforts, however, often lost money for New Directions, and, from the beginning, Laughlin compensated losses with his own funds.

MacNiven's biography is enlivened by reports of Laughlin's encounters with figures vital to twentieth century literature: the arch elitist Vladimir Nabokov, the sweet devotional simplicity of Thomas Merton, the impecunious Dylan Thomas, who complained that his family had no money for food, the irascible and often contentious Kenneth Rexroth, who took him hiking in the high Sierras and reinforced his interest in Asian literature, the explosive and sometimes delusional Delmore Schwartz, who helped run New Directions for a time.

Laughlin possessed considerable grace, civility, and intelligence, rare qualities in his world. He was a towering eminence in American publishing, and not just because he was almost six and a half feet tall. An avid skier, who developed a resort in Utah, who traveled in socially prominent circles, Laughlin was passionate about poetry, wrote it himself quite skillfully, and at one point, caught in the folly of youthful literary idealism, drove around the United States with a car full of books, trying to peddle the little known writers whose books he had published in local bookstores.

There was as much sadness in Laughlin's life as dedication and accomplishment—marital incompatibilities, the suicide of a son at twenty-seven, his own fear that he had inherited his father's bipolarity. To his credit, MacNiven does not sensationalize the troubles, though some readers may regard as unnecessary his insistence on recording so much of the minutia of publishing. However, the details are relevant: Laughlin was devoted to his literature and served his writers. He remained "a lifelong friend of lost literary souls," he admitted in 1993, four years before his death at eighty-three.

Renegade Rosset

> Congress shall make no law respecting an establishment of religion, or prohibiting the free exercise thereof; or abridging the freedom of speech, or of the press; or the right of the people peaceably to assemble, and to petition the Government for a redress of grievances.

Opinionated, irascible, brazen but smart, a gutsy dynamo of American alternative publishing, Barney Rosset was a 130 pound bantamweight on amphetamines, with a bear's loyal heart and stubbornness, a rum and coke man who often forgot about the need for food to accompany his drinks at lunch.

His mother was a descendant of Irish tenant farmers whose land was mostly peat bog that they used as a sort of low-grade fuel. The Tansley family used Gaelic as code and was involved in a clandestine struggle in nineteenth century Ireland, part of an underclass subject to the exploitation of Anglo-Irish aristocrats who actually owned the land. Rosset's red-headed mother, working as a bank teller in Chicago, met and married Barnet Rosset, the son of Russian Jews from Moscow, who so excelled at accounting that he administered a succession of small banks.

An only child, Barney was indulged, sent to progressive schools, and despite the ravages of the Great Depression, he was the first kid in his fancy high school to own his own automobile. In 1940, he spent his freshman year of college at

Swarthmore, not because of any commitment to the Quaker values stressed at that institution, but because he wanted to stay close to a girl he had fallen in love with in high school. He felt stultified as a student, but compensated for his boredom with academic proprieties in an autodidactic manner:

> I had always been drawn to books that were considered risky. When I was at Swarthmore in 1940, I asked my parents to send me 50 books, all of which were published by New Directions or the Modern Library. And before that, when I was in Chicago attending high school, I went to Marshall Field & Co. to get books by John Steinbeck, James Farrell, and other writers considered too daring to read.

One of the books that most intrigued him was a book of essays, Henry Miller's *The Cosmological Eye* that had been just published by James Laughlin at New Directions. This was where Rosset first learned about Miller's banned novel, *Tropic of Cancer*. He discovered a copy of a pirated edition in Frances Steloff's Gotham Book Mart in Manhattan—she sold him a copy that she kept under the counter. Rosset was drawn to Miller's attacks on conformity and wrote a paper for his English class, "Henry Miller Versus Our Way of Life." His professor, the distinguished literary historian Robert Spiller, rewarded him with a B-. Probably speaking for the entire country at the time, Spiller pronounced that Miller was jaundiced, but the impact of *Tropic of Cancer* would linger.

Rosset then decided to study film at U.C.L.A until he enlisted in the military in 1942. His father helped him get into O.C.S., and he was stationed in Astoria, New York to study film production. The experience was formative, and he responded fully to the "immediate connection" he felt while filming, learning to edit as he shot. Up to this point his story is a humdrum *bildungsroman* of privileged youth, frustrated courtships, and dissatisfaction with the prospects before him. When he was sent to China, conditions became more precarious and tense:

> After waiting at an airbase, a steaming hole, for two days, I boarded one of the ungainly, underpowered C-46s for the plane ride over the Himalayas to China. Taking off from Assam, India, for Kunming, my unit's Chinese HQ, in December of 1944, I was still a raw, semi-trained second lieutenant in the Signal Corps Photographic Service, 22 years old and with only a few dreams to cling to. Squashed under the weight of my equipment, I struggled onto the airplane and sat on the metal floor next to some uncommunicative Chinese soldiers. I leaned back in the curve of the bare fuselage, hugging a heavy parachute, which was a totally foreign object to me. We were in a death crate, a hulk of a cargo plane barely sustained by two undersized motors. As we puffed oxygen through our masks, the planet's highest mountains glowered beneath us and loomed on both sides.

Japanese Zeroes shadow the C-46, using it as cover to strafe the landing field. Driving a small truck on unpaved roads, Rosset was dispatched to the Sino-Japanese front, near Kweiyang, to replace an officer who had committed suicide and to document the Japanese retreat. The description of his activities as a photographer behind enemy lines in China is as graphic, hellish, and intense, really, as Norman Mailer's more capacious accounts in *The Naked and the Dead.* It is the most gripping part of the book.

During the war, Rosset fought in a *white* army. Under the prevalent doctrine of "separate but equal," African-Americans were as segregated on the field of battle as they were in the neighborhood housing of America. After the war, Rosset produced *Strange Victory,* a film about race relations that compared the deplorable American situation with that of Nazi Germany. The film failed to get much attention even though it was a breakthrough attempt to explore the subject. The experience discouraged Rosset from a filmmaking career and—perhaps as a sign of how considerably he had been crushed by its poor reception—the film doesn't receive much treatment from Rosset himself.

He began taking classes at The New School with prominent teachers, like Wallace Fowlie, Stanley Kunitz, Meyer Schapiro, and Alfred Kazin. He also married the Abstract Expressionist painter, Joan Mitchell, whom he had known since prep school, and he spent much of 1949 with her in France and Spain. Except for the inclusion of a few of her letters to him, we are given little access to the union or the reasons for its collapse in 1952.

Prodded by Joan Mitchell, and with three thousand dollars provided by his father, Rosset bought a small start-up reprint house called Grove Press, because it was located at 18 Grove Street in the West Village. With it, he would change the genteel decorum of American publishing with a contentious, political, street savvy perspective, quite absent from the more polite protocols of conventional publishing.

Rosset would remain in the Village for most of the rest of his long life—he died at 89, in 2012—and his evocative abilities excel when recapturing the flavor of the Village in the 1950s:

> Going out from our narrow entrance lane and turning left on Eleventh Street, you came in less than a block to Seventh Avenue and the Village Vanguard. We got to know Max Gordon, the proprietor, and his wife, Lorraine, very well. We spent hours at the Vanguard with the likes of Pete Seeger and his folk group. One night the great South African singer Miriam Makeba came on stage, fresh from the slums of Soweto and Johannesburg. It was at the Vanguard we saw

the tragicomic Lenny Bruce warning us there was a cop in a raincoat in the audience; and then Miles Davis playing his horn facing the wall one night because the audience annoyed him; Jack Kerouac spinning a bizarre, more than slightly drunk monologue; and Huddie Ledbetter, Lead Belly himself, just out of a Southern prison, escorted by Alan Lomax, singing his new song "Goodnight, Irene."

For Rosset, publishers were "foot soldiers in the struggle against hypocrisy and oppression." In the service of what he regarded as a mission to voice the priorities of personal freedom, he published the work of European writers such as Bertold Brecht, Antonin Artaud, Jean Genet, and Samuel Beckett. Inspired writers, who had seen their work rejected by every mainstream press, could hope for an audience through Rosset, who believed that a publisher should *affect* the culture, change it rather than merely reflect its dominant values.

No American publisher was as dedicated to publishing drama, the avant-garde, the unknown but sexually provocative writers, like Hubert Selby. Except for James Laughlin, who provided a model, no American publisher was as dedicated to translations of foreign writers. To further this effort to overcome American provinciality, one of his editors, Richard Seaver, was fluent in French and another, Fred Jordon, in German. Rosset had met Seaver in Paris in 1949, when Seaver was translating Beckett, who was then writing in French. Seaver would be instrumental in Rosset's acquisition of *Waiting for Godot* (with the ridiculous advance of one hundred and fifty dollars!) and Jean Genet's *The Maids* in 1954, plays that transformed theater.

Two events near the end of the 1950s seemed indicative of Rosset's intention to shake up the smug complacencies of what was called the Silent Generation. In 1957, he began The *Evergreen Review*, a national magazine that was always willing to challenge the status quo, which published Kerouac, Ginsberg,

Ferlinghetti, Gary Snyder, Michael McClure, Norman Mailer, and Charles Bukowski. At the same time, Rosset published an anthology called *The New American Poetry* that was dominated by the work of Beat poets using the "open form" that shook the academic formalism of the poetry establishment and shocked its sense of poetic decorum. The book made a lasting impression on the nature of American poetics and its future.

Two years later, Rosset published the unexpurgated edition of D.H. Lawrence's *Lady Chatterley's Lover*, the Orioli edition that had been published in Italy in 1928, but was banned everywhere else. The court battle, aided by the sympathetic testimony of witnesses, like critics Malcolm Cowley and Alfred Kazin, resulted in the sale of over one million copies of Lawrence's novel, and established a clear precedent as to what could be published in America.

Rosset's profound impact on American culture in the 1960s was perhaps best reflected in his determination to publish the first legitimate American edition of Henry Miller's banned novel, *Tropic of Cancer*. Thanks to the agency of Anaïs Nin, who supported Miller and subsidized the printing costs for his novel, Miller's novel had been published in 1934 in Paris by the Olympia Press, a firm with a dubious reputation because of its pornographic list. His novel was considered contraband; "proscribed" was the official term used by American customs authorities for the next few decades.

Rosset approached Miller in the spring of 1959. Grove was publishing sixty to seventy titles annually at that point, yet it was still condescended to by the larger uptown firms. Miller lived in a log cabin on Big Sur in California, supporting himself marginally on the occasional sale of a watercolor. He was content with his disreputable reputation as an outlaw author, whose books were smuggled into the United States, mostly by G.I.s returning from European duty after the Second World War. Reluctant to authorize an American edition, Miller was ambivalent about fame, and feared a predictable and protracted court wrangle. He warned Rosset about an edition of his book, printed illicitly in Mexico, which had been distributed by a salacious book dealer named Jack Brussel, an act that got Brussel incarcerated in a federal penitentiary in Pennsylvania for three years.

Miller became a personal mission for Rosset. He would spend a quarter of a million dollars in legal fees to establish the right to publish *Tropic of Cancer* in America, willing to gamble the entire future of Grove on the potential hazards. He persuaded Miller with a huge advance of $50,000, an unheard of amount at that time.

The court contest for the right to publish *Tropic of Cancer* was epic in scope. Rosset had to hire two dozen attorneys to represent him in some sixty lower court proceedings, all of which were decided against Grove Press. Next was an even more expensive challenge in five State Supreme Courts. The judicial process lasted for two years and generated a lot of free publicity. The trials ended with the United States Supreme Court decision allowing Rosset to publish the book, enlarging forever the notion of what one was free to write and publish. That 5 to 4 decision of the Warren Court, like Brown vs. Board of Education, an earlier one that ended a century of American apartheid, changed the face and future of America. No wonder Eisenhower regretted his nomination of Earl Warren—who had formerly been the conservative Republican governor of California—to head the court. Justice Warren had been the swing vote in both cases.

Miller can be considered the spiritual granddaddy of the Beat Generation, and Rosset was ready to publish key works like Michael McClure's play *The Beard*, or Jack Kerouac's *Doctor Sax* and *The Subterraneans*. The decision to print *The Subterraneans*—a novel describing a love affair between a white protagonist and an African-American woman—was particularly brave. Although *The Subterraneans* escaped the censors in the U.S., it was prosecuted as pornography in Italy. Rosset was the sole witness for the defense, which ultimately prevailed. Rosset also had enough moxie to publish William Burroughs' *Naked Lunch* in 1962, a book that was more overtly descriptive of sexual circumstance than Kerouac's, and

Burroughs' book would only be fully exonerated by the highest court of Massachusetts in 1966.

The turbulent 1960s certainly affected the frenzy of activity at Grove Press. As Rosset admitted in a letter to Samuel Beckett, his "head seemed like packages of wires ripped open and twisted, misconnected and short-circuited. Sometimes a message reaches some center, only to get annihilated on its way to the next."

All through the 1970s, Grove's fortunes began to decline. His publishing career had always been acrobatically poised on the verge of bankruptcy, according to Lois Oppenheim, the editor of *Dear Mr. Becket,* a charming book about the friendship of Rosset and Beckett. Rosset sold a lot of land he had purchased in East Hampton to finance the press but prospects became grim. His staff was diminished from 35 employees to nine, and in the years 1971-2 alone, the firm lost eight million dollars. This was a period of conglomerate mergers in the face of a general decline in publishing revenue. Rosset also lost a lot of money producing films like Norman Mailer's *Maidstone*, which turned out to be a production disaster with one of the actors threatening Mailer. Rosset first went public and then, in 1985, sold his firm to Anne Getty, of the oil fortune, and Lord George Weidenfeld, an English publisher, with the provision that he remain as editor-in-chief. A year later, in what proved to be a pattern in publishing, he was betrayed and "they would wind up ousting [him] without ceremony."

Rosset started a small press, Blue Moon Books, and began work on a memoir. In 1998, I interviewed him in connection with my own hybrid memoir, *Paradise Outlaws.* He told me that one of his last acts—right before he had been fired—had been to reprint *Naked Angels.* Grove succeeded in keeping my book in print for another few decades.

I can testify that to the end of his long life he still smiled like a rogue and drank prodigiously. "For God's sake don't give up drink," he admonished Beckett. "Ex-drinkers are more than I can put up with." He remained thin, lively, always engaged in the new. As Paul Auster has aptly characterized him in his rambling preface to *Dear Mr. Beckett,* Barney was "the youngest old man in America." But he struggled with how to tell his own story. Although he had lost none of his acuity, and could still drink me under the table, Barney was easily fatigued and had lost some of his stamina and fire.

His memoir reflects this. *My Life in Publishing* is something of a composite. Rosset worked on it too long, with various assistants and editors, but was never fully satisfied and kept eliminating what he had written. Is it a sign of a lack of confidence in his own power to articulate, or were his expectations too great? This version integrates letters and other previously rejected sections his editors found in archives at Columbia University and material, like an essay on Beckett that Rosset wrote for another purpose. Suddenly, in the middle of his memoir, there are a dozen letters exchanged between Beckett and Rosset on the problems in translating *Waiting for Godot* into an American idiom. While this might interest a specialist in Beckett, it has less appeal for a general audience.

Rosset's account may not be as exemplary as the actual record of achievement. While editors are frequently writers, they are often forced to devote their concentration to another's writing, often frustrated by the lack of opportunity to develop their own creativity. Sometimes the book is digressive, occasionally it meanders. Sometimes what is inserted in the text—like an O.S.S. report on his disqualification for service in that secret branch of shadow governance—seems awkward or extraneous, perhaps useful in an appendix (and I should note there are four appended sections which each add value).

Occasionally, Rosset reminisces about women he had pursued unsuccessfully, or recalls past lovers, but such snatches are undeveloped. We learn almost nothing about his lifetime as a psychoanalytic subject or the emotional reasons for the collapse of his marriage to Joan Mitchell, and nothing at all about the five marriages that followed. Serial marriage is a male American pattern, but it needs more explanation than innuendo. Memoir depends on selectivity, but this sort of omission seems like vagueness or evasion.

He provides much more intimately intriguing detail with friends like Jackson Pollock and Beckett, and we get close observation of Beckett's domestic arrangements—even the night in Paris when Rosset had to share a bed in his hotel room with Beckett—and the occasion of losing Beckett, who was on his last trip to New York at the World's Fair in Flushing, and then finding him sound asleep like a character in *Godot* on a park bench! Such rich anecdotes may be more entertaining for the general reader than chapters detailing legal strategies for the defense of *Lady Chatterley's Lover* or *Tropic of Cancer*.

I suspect, at the end, he was profoundly discouraged by the loss of Grove, which would merge with Atlantic, and sacrifice every bit of the loudly outspoken, radical character he had created for his firm over three decades. *My Life in Publishing* becomes a sort of justification, a history of giant achievement, in changing popular taste and welcoming the new, but at the expense of the emotional truth that makes any memoir sing.

Lawrence Ferlinghetti's Walkabout

> But you, a new brood, native, athletic,
>   continental, greater than before known,
> Arouse! for you must justify me.
>
> --Walt Whitman, "Poets to Come"

It is commonplace, though often denied by romantic humanists, that technology has a formative impact on life as we know it. Of course, the habit of reading—a book, newspaper, or this essay—depends upon technological innovation. A German goldsmith named Johannes Gensfleisch Gutenberg designed a printing system on a wine press using movable metal type in a small, dark room in the medieval town of Mainz in 1455. The cultural consequences of Gutenberg's printing press led to the reproduction of classical texts—driving what we call the Renaissance—and allowed the possibility of democratic governance that depends on people getting the news.

    In the American colonies, approximately three hundred years later, small, independent printing establishments could enable a printer, like James Franklin, to diminish the stranglehold of Cotton Mather and the Puritan theocracy in

Boston, or pamphleteer Thomas Paine in New York to get the word of *Common Sense* and *The Rights of Man* to farming folk in the back country. These were revolutionary developments. As late as the middle of the nineteenth century, a former journalist named Walt Whitman found a press in Brooklyn on which he could set the type of "Song of Myself"—the first long poem, free of all classical or European models, that could be called characteristically American.

All this is history, perhaps, but it matters in so far as the contemporary literary situation is concerned. This is an age when smaller publishers have been forced to collapse their trade divisions or be swallowed whole by big publishers who consolidate to form a few giant conglomerates, mostly owned by European entities like Pearson, Hachette, or Bertelsmann.

In such a moment, perilous for American readers and writers alike actually, the presence of alternative small-presses (and on-line publication as well) have been both vital and potentially viral. One model for enduring small-press success has been the publishing entity City Lights in San Francisco, founded and formed by the poet Lawrence Ferlinghetti in 1955.

Major cultural changes often result from individual vocation and choices. Ferlinghetti's life story seems so characteristically American. He had a rocky beginning in life: his Italian father died six months before his birth and his French mother was sent to an asylum a few months later. Fortunately, he was adopted by the daughter of the man who founded Sarah Lawrence College and was raised in Bronxville, an elite suburb north of New York City. He was sent to prep schools, and, at the University of North Carolina at Chapel Hill, he wrote on sports for *The Daily Tarheel,* and contributed stories to *The Carolina Quarterly*, an excellent literary magazine.

Enlisting in the Navy after Pearl Harbor, he served as an officer on sub chasers, escort vessels that dropped explosives on German submarines. He participated in the invasion of Normandy, which was the beginning of the defeat of Germany, and felt impelled to visit Nagasaki six weeks after the atomic explosion that ended the war with Japan. On the G.I. Bill, he studied at Columbia University, and then went to France in 1947 to study at the Sorbonne, where he received a doctorate. In 1951, in San Francisco, he began working with Peter Martin on his magazine, *City Lights*, named after Chaplin's film, and where Ferlinghetti's first translations of the French Resistance poet Jacques Prevert appeared.

With Martins, Ferlinghetti started a paperbound bookstore, a novel idea after the war, as the book market was changing. Located between North Beach and Chinatown, City Lights was intended as a place to foster intellectual inquiry and activity. He also created a press that, like Barney Rosset's Grove Press, was based on the notion that freedom of speech needed advocacy. One of its focal points became Beat-related publications, like *The Yagé Letters*, an epistolary exchange between Burroughs and Ginsberg from the Amazon basin, and Neal Cassady's *The First Third*, an awkward, strained account of the Beat catalyst's early years.

Ferlinghetti wanted to publish poetry in an inexpensive format that could reach working classes, rather than the more elite audience that patronized poetry. The Pocket Poets Series issued funny looking little square paperbacks that could be easily carried in a pocket. The first book he published in this series was his own, *Pictures of a Gone World*, a hand assembled letterpress edition of 500 copies, a mixture of elegy and optimism influenced by the modernist anticipations of Apollinaire, Prevert, and e.e. cummings. The fourth slim volume in the Pocket Books Series was Ginsberg's *Howl and Other Poems* (1956), an explosion of form and content that changed the nature of American poetry and had to be vindicated by judicial process in order to appear in print at all.

Like Ginsberg, Ferlinghetti's poetry reacts to a rote academic formalism, and he seems inspired more by raucous sounds of the street than hushed whispers in a museum. His choices for the Pocket Poets Series at City Lights seem guided by a sense of linguistic freedom influenced more by the way we actually speak in the heat of the moment than the manner in which past poets have put words on paper. The tradition of what should be called "natural speech," begun by Whitman, is exemplified by the remark of William Carlos Williams, who told Allen Ginsberg the story of doing his rounds by car as a pediatrician in Paterson, New Jersey, when he heard two laborers arguing in a ditch. One of them shouted "I'll kick yuh in yer eye!" which became a hallmark of the immediacy, directness, and emotional honesty Williams wanted to capture in his poems.

As the neurologist, Oliver Sachs, pointed out in a column in *The New York Times*, shortly before his death, the spoken word, as opposed to the more controlled written version, tends to be more open, improvised, unpredictable, spontaneous, and ultimately inventive. For the most part, the poems in the 60th anniversary edition of the *City Lights Anthology of Pocket Poets* live up to Williams' fresh, irrepressible expectations.

The disadvantage of any anthology, however, is that it can provide more of a particular taste than the sustenance of a substantial meal. While the result often may not fully represent the poet, it can serve an editor's priorities. From the beginning of the series in 1955, Ferlinghetti's intention was to provoke, to discover unknown new voices, to create an "international, dissident, insurgent ferment," to challenge the political (or economic) given, the safe assumptions of a culture that seemed bound by its affluence and commodities. A good illustration exists early in the anthology, with the Moloch section of Ginsberg's "Howl":

> Moloch whose eyes are a thousand blind windows!
> Moloch whose skyscrapers stand in the long streets like endless Jehovahs! Moloch whose factories dream and croak in the fog! Moloch whose smoke-stacks and antennae crown the cities!
>
> Moloch whose love is endless oil and stone! Moloch whose soul is electricity and banks! Moloch

> whose poverty is the specter of genius! Moloch
> whose fate is a cloud of sexless hydrogen!
> Moloch whose name is the Mind!

For Ginsberg, the Canaanite god, Moloch, to whom children were sacrificed in pre-biblical times, stands for the inequities of a capitalist system. The pronounced rhythmic hammer of the exclamation point that recurs some eighty-five times in the two page Moloch section of the poem, is typical of the rage that Ginsberg releases in the first half of "Howl." The tone of the poem shifts drastically after the Moloch section, however, and the Footnote coda that Ferlinghetti includes—with its perplexingly haunting reiteration of the word "holy"—reflects the turn to the magnanimity of Ginsberg's perspective, the sublimity and largesse of his conception.

There is a lot more of Ginsberg in the anthology, especially since eight of Ginsberg's poetry collections appeared with the Pocket Poets imprint. While many of the selections cannot match the intensity of "Howl," there is a selection from *Kaddish*, the elegy Ginsberg wrote to his mother, perhaps his second most powerful and anguished poem, and a fragment of a key breakthrough dream poem, "Siesta in Xbalba," written just prior to "Howl," when Ginsberg was living in Chiapas, Mexico.

City Lights has always been key to the dissemination of Beat literature. Except for the early success of *Howl and Other Poems* and *On the Road*, the Beats were unpopular through the 1970s, belittled by *Time-Life* publications, and frequently condescended to in places like *The New York Times*. The reputations of writers like Kerouac and Burroughs only began to change drastically in the 1990s with a Whitney Museum show and events like the LACMA show of William Burroughs' shotgun paintings. Ferlinghetti was first in America to publish Jack Kerouac's poems as number 28 in the Pocket Poets Series, and in this volume he includes poems like the brilliant "How to Meditate" and "Hymn," with its stunning prediction of Kerouac's own brief transit on this planet:

Beat Transnationalism

> So whatever plan you have for me
> Splitter of majesty
> Make it short
> brief
> Make it snappy
> bring me home to the Eternal Mother
> today
>
> At your service anyway,
> (and until)

The Beat movement is often still limited to the success of a few figures, like Ginsberg, Kerouac (who declared it was over long before "Howl"), and Burroughs (who denied participation, anyway). I've never done an actuarial count but my estimate is that there are at least one hundred writers who should be included. Some of them, like Gregory Corso, Bob Kaufman, Philip Lamantia, Jack Hirshman, and Ginsberg's companion, Peter Orlovsky, with his *Clean Asshole Poems & Smiling Vegetable Songs* forming number 37 in the Pocket Poets Series are represented here, as well as some neo-Beats, like Harold Norse, Frank O'Hara, Denise Levertov, Robert Bly, and David Meltzer.

And even though the Beats early on got the reputation of existing as an all-boy gang, there were a number of women involved, including: Joyce Johnson, Hettie Jones, Bonnie Bremser, Janine Pommy-Vega, Anne Waldman, and Diane Di Prima (whose account of bathing simultaneously with Kerouac and Ginsberg is one of high points of Beat hilarity, like Robert Frank's film, "Pull My Daisy"). Di Prima, Pommy-Vega and Waldman all appeared in Pocket Poet editions, and, consequently, some of their work is represented here.

However, the anthology is not another Beat collection like Ann Charters' *Portable Beat Reader* or Anne Waldman's *The Beat Book*. From the start, part of Ferlinghetti's plan was international in scope to counter American insularity and provinciality, the planetary isolation caused before the age of aviation by the comfort of oceanic protection on each side of the continent. In the United States, no other publisher, with the exception of James Laughlin at New Directions or Barney Rosset at Grove, has been as dedicated to translation and the awareness that literature resonates on a transnational plane. So, a good part of the anthology includes work by such writers as Pablo Neruda, Federico Garcia Lorca, and Antonio Machado (all translated by Kenneth Rexroth, an early figure on the San Francisco Beat scene), Nicanor Parra, Ernesto Cardenal, Jacques Prevert, Pier Pasolini, and Russian writers, like Andrei Voznesensky, Yevgeny Yevtushenko, and Vladimir Mayakovsky.

Not all of the figures represented in the anthology fall into the Beat or international categories. Perhaps my favorite moments in the book are provided by the delicately nuanced lyrics of Marie Ponsot (who met Ferlinghetti in 1945 on a ship returning from France) or Malcolm Lowry, best known for *Under the Volcano,* his dark, infernal novel of Conradian descent. Indeed, one of the brief poems included here is entitled "Joseph Conrad" and is as much about the seaman's life as the poet's "struggling with the form/Of his coiled work." Lowry's wrenched, wrestling poems of existential suffering, like the "Death of a Oaxaquenian," which revolves around the refrain of "So huge is God's despair," ring with the power of John Donne's Holy Sonnets.

The true marvel of the *City Light Pocket Poets Anthology* is its reappearance in its sixtieth year. That represents a venerable tradition (and a long run) for an avant-garde that often mutates too quickly for continuity. A decade ago, I was invited to a bibliophile's paradise, the Grolier Club in Manhattan, to view a collection of the chapbooks in the Pocket Poets Series, owned by a Chicago headhunter. It was a swanky affair, with the waiters passing trays of the most delectable hors d'oeuvres and enough cocktails to stagger Dylan Thomas. Some of the invited guests were talking about Yeats manuscripts, others about the latest folio discovery—the Shakespeare hunt now four hundred years old. I suspect the event cost more than the production of any of the Pocket books, and it probably added up to more than any sum realized by any of the poets who were represented.

The Beats are slipping into history, although there are a few second-generation survivors, like Anne Waldman or David Meltzer, and a few active original collaborators left, like the musician, David Amram, or the photographer, Robert Frank. Ferlinghetti is ninety-seven, but he is still writing engaged poems, as politically and progressively inclined as ever. New Directions recently published his *Time of Useful Consciousness*, the second part of a longer work in progress called *Americus*. Just as Ginsberg's *Howl and Other Poems* became the best-selling poetry book of a generation, Ferlinghetti's own *A Coney Island of the Mind*, with its insouciant bravado and cheer, has passed the million sales mark. That's a rare occurrence in these United States.

So are the Pocket Poets Series and the continuance of City Lights Press. Ferlinghetti's intention—in the tradition of the French *engage* writer, like Camus or Sartre—was always to provoke, to discover unknown new voices, to challenge the political (or economic) given, the comfortable assumptions of a culture that seemed bound by its affluence and commodities. City Lights Press became the model for a small-press alternative in America. This was important at a time when bigger, more commercial publishers were selling their assets to Europeans, collapsing their trade divisions, consolidating or disappearing.

II.

I suppose the most surprising thing about Lawrence Ferlinghetti is that, at the age of 97, he is still writing engaged poems. Ferlinghetti's poems have usually reflected his life, but the recently published journals in *Writing Across the Landscape* offer a fuller view.

Artisans and Impresarios

Some of *Writing Across the Landscape* is the result of Ferlinghetti's publishing efforts, "tracking down some author for an undiscovered masterpiece," or reading his own work at poetry festivals in Amsterdam, Berlin, Paris, or Mexico City. These travel journals were drawn from unpublished handwritten notebooks in the Bancroft Library at the University of California at Berkeley. At the same time, this record seems to be a process of rediscovering his own European roots in the tradition of D.H. Lawrence's sojourns in Italy and Mexico.

Perhaps the most astonishing, yet characteristically powerful entry in *Writing Across the Landscape* occurs in a journal of February, 1967, when Ferlinghetti (inspired by a book by Blaise Cendrars) crosses Russia on the Trans-Siberian Railway, the longest rail ride in the world. An eight day trip, his cabin heated by coal to 45 degrees, he traverses through empty space with "nothing but birch trees like the froth on endless white groundswells," and an occasional town. "There is an enormous emptiness in Soviet life that stares out of people's eyes everywhere," he observes. No one on the train smiled, and the loudspeaker in the corridor blasted *Figaro* in Russian: "It's like listening to a stuck bull roaring."

Reaching the Sea of Japan, waiting for a ship to convey him to Kyoto where he intends to visit Gary Snyder, he remembers a time over two decades earlier when he was the navigator on an attack transport, the *U.S.S. Selinur*. His ship had docked in Sasebo, a few hours south of Nagasaki when, with a few shipmates, he took a train to the scorched earth site of a city that had vanished "except for one tea cup with bottom melted out." The event is presented with a minimum of detail, understated, I suppose, because language often becomes insufficient in the face of death and catastrophe. Now, he writes, he sees the bombing as a "monstrous racist act" which would never have been committed had the Japanese had white skin. What is remarkable about the entry, to me, is not the driven nail of this judgment, but the fact that Ferlinghetti understood in 1945 that the instantaneous erasure of an entire city was something (despite the radiation exposure) that obligated a poet to bear witness.

Another entry that moved me especially was Ferlinghetti's account of seeing Ezra Pound for the first time at the Spoleto Festival in 1965. The giant of modernism was sitting next to his mistress, Olga Rudge, "still as a mandarin statue" in a box in a theater balcony, "thin and long-haired, aquiline at eighty, head tilted strangely to one side, lost in permanent abstraction..." After an hour, when it was Pound's turn to read, he was unable to rise from his balcony seat, so he read from his seated position:

> First the jaw moved and then the voice came out, inaudible. A young Italian pulled up the mike very close to his face and held it there, and the voice came over, frail but stubborn, higher than I had expected, a thin, soft monotone... The hall had gone silent at a stroke. The voice knocked me down, so soft, so thin, so frail, so stubborn still. I put my head on my arms on the velvet sill of the box. I was surprised to see a single tear drop on my knee. The thin, indomitable voice went on. I went blind from the box into the empty corridor of the theater where they still sat turned to him, went down and out, into the sunlight, weeping...

Three decades later, Ferlinghetti finds himself wandering around Dorsoduro, the neighborhood in Venice, where Pound spent his last years in a deliberate silence with Olga Rudge. Venice, Ferlinghetti notes, is the place for the *deracines, the* alienated *frustrati*, the ones who do not fit, the jilted lovers, and all the romantics of the world. It is the place of Pound's final slumber: "the deep sleep of the confused Confucian... Aye, but the great sounds he could emit!"

Another section of this commodious book that particularly interested me was the account of a series of trips Ferlinghetti took to Oaxaca, Guadalajara, San Miguel de Allendes, and various other Mexican locations. "Pardon me if I disappear in Mexico," he begins his narrative, "wearing a mask and strange suspenders." His characteristic humor, usually genial and Chaplinesque, here is often warped by the desolation and poverty he sees:

> Passing through Tijuana, I see legless man at downtown dirt corner sitting in backseat of antique sedan from which doors have been torn. He has stained felt hat on center of head, rimless eyeglasses with cracked glass, a huge old typewriter propped up before him on wood box. Typing, he has butt of cigarette stuck to lower lip, burnt-out Signs hung on car say:
> ESCRITOR PUBLICO
> A campesino speaks to him from the curb; he writes what he hears....legless, he holds the mirror up.

It is a brilliant vignette, compassionate, full of the heart of sorrow, as well as a projection of the kind of writing he finds more useful in the world.

His view, very much like what Kerouac tried to do with his romantic view of the Mexican Fellaheen in *On the Road*, anticipates the multi-culturalism that was such a strong feature of Beat camaraderie from the beginning. It is what enabled poets, like LeRoi Jones in New York and Bob Kaufmann in San Francisco, to identify with Ginsberg and Kerouac.

Consider the passage where he imagines the end of all border controls that he includes shortly after he sees the legless writer, in the border town of Mexicali:

> Nothing to stop the hordes of the world still starving and howling like Calibans at the gates, no customs, no wars, no protective no passports, and naturalization papers, none of the old protective barriers...leaving no alternative but

to recognize the Indians as brothers…the whole earth blended into one skin with one tongue. It will only take 5000 more years to do this.

This sort of universalism, which seems precariously threatened in the Age of Terrorism, is a cornerstone of a Beat politics, which is not usually reflected by conventional views. As Ferlinghetti once observed, the Democratic Party in the U.S. is like an eagle with two right wings. Its spirit is captured in a fantasy-caricature bus ride, he imagines in a 1917 bus whose destination is written above the driver's front window: REVOLUCION DIRECTO. The bus is full of diplomats in tuxedos, all smoking cigars and blowing their noses into little American flag handkerchiefs. One is using the flag to wipe the semen he has just ejaculated. There is a parrot on the driver's head calling out the stops. Soon, the bus gets very very crowded, and the diplomats each have an old woman, Indian or beggar, seated on their laps. In Ferlinghetti's parody, the diplomats are engaged in fellatio, letting out curious cries and then mopping up with their handkerchief flags. The bus careens to a stop in front of some Latin American embassy where it is showered by guano, and the flags are now "pressed into service spontaneously in a new great mopping-up operation gumshoe." The entire episode, which goes on for pages, is hilarious, but bitter parody. It is political, just as the poet e.e. cummings, Burroughs, or Ginsberg understood that politicians (and diplomats are their cousins), as a species, are shit-eaters who wish to live like lords at our expense.

Writing Against the Landscape offers many passages as intriguing as the ones I've selected. While some readers may complain that the geography of "landscape" is subordinated to a more spiritually derived sense of the character of a place, often more like succinct visual reveries than sustained analytical probing, Ferlinghetti's descriptions are offered as an accumulating procession of minute particulars, presented with a lyrical clarity and natural ease throughout his narrative:

Artisans and Impresarios

It is strange sitting in this Italian landscape, watching the swallows wheel over a back garden in Spoleto, the morning sun over the hills in the distance, the sky hot white-blue, stone house & tile roofs, fig trees, washing hung out on the iron railings of the balcony on which I am sitting. Singing birds in cages in the garden awoke me.

This is a large, magnanimous book, written with a wide angle lens that spans from 1944 to 2010, and there are so many evocative moments included, signs of the "Coca-colonization" in Peru, Mexico, Cuba, and Nicaragua, at the barricades during the uprising of students in Paris in 1968, in Italy to find his father's birthplace in Brescia, in Germany, in Fiji, Tahiti, Australia—all stops on what he calls his "walkabout in the world."

Acknowledgements:

I wish to thank Daniel Shapiro at the Americas Society, who encouraged me to speak to the issue of Beat Mexico, which initiated this book. An early version of my first chapter appeared in *Studies in Latin American Popular Culture* in 2013. The essay on "Howl" first appeared in *The Antioch Review* in 2015. Michael Ursell and Tom Lutz at the *Los Angeles Review of Books* have welcomed my essays, and the piece on Judith Malina began on their pages and in *Artforum*. Bruce Falconer at *The American Scholar* has been equally receptive, and he asked me to write the piece on James Laughlin. The essays in Oliver Harris and Ian MacFadyen's useful anthology, *Naked Lunch @ 50,* helped to broaden my perspective on Beat studies. John Morgenstern at Clemson University Press suggested I write the essay on the transnational character of Beat writing. My wife Mellon, my editor David S. Wills, Joyce Johnson, Bill Morgan, Nancy Grace, and Jeffrey Di Leo have also encouraged my literary efforts in various ways.